To Michael —

Make the future!

Bob Shearer

More Praise for *Leaders Make the Future*

"What wonderful timing! Bob Johansen has given us cause for optimism by providing leaders from all sectors with sound and practical advice to weather the uncertainty and volatility around us."

—BOB IVANY, Former Commandant, US Army War College

"*Leaders Make the Future* is the right book for these challenging times. Using an exciting combination of insights from foresight, as well as systems and design thinking, he has succeeded in clearly describing the essential skills leaders must use to thrive in our world of volatility, uncertainty, complexity, and ambiguity—the VUCA world."

—BRADLEY A. PERKINS, MD, MBA, Chief Strategy and Innovation
Officer, Centers for Disease Control and Prevention

"Bob Johansen focuses on how leaders can make decisions and perform when the pace of decision making and its consequences in our interdependent world have never been greater. *Leaders Make the Future* provides an analytical and operational framework for decision making in the VUCA soup."   —THOMAS H. GLOCER, CEO, Thomson Reuters

"Nonprofits will be stretched by the future in frightening ways. *Leaders Make the Future* gives inspiration and practical advice to nonprofit leaders as we struggle to make the future a better place for all."

—STEPHEN BENNETT, President and CEO, United Cerebral Palsy

"Bob Johansen offers clear and inspiring guideposts to deal with profound leadership challenges that face us in the 21st century. Leaders take note: you will need both strategy *and* learning, expressed with great clarity. This book is an important call to action."

—WILLIE PIETERSEN, Professor, The Practice of Management,
Columbia Business School

"Bob Johansen, with his decades of experience in forecasting, sets out the critical skills leaders must use not only to make sense of today but to truly shape the future. Any aspiring leader would benefit from this study on becoming a positive agent for change and determining what kind of future one wants to create."

—BRIAN DAVISON, Vice President, Strategic Planning, Kraft Foods

"Johansen offers both steps to strengthen our skills as well as insights to inspire us to build a better future. It is the must-read partner to his other recent book, *Get There Early*."

—JEAN McCLUNG HALLORAN, Senior Vice President,
Human Resources, Agilent Technologies

"The health-care industry is squarely in the VUCA world. *Leaders Make the Future* provides a powerfully relevant glimpse of the leadership skills necessary for organizations to flourish in this new reality and should be required reading for all health-care executive teams."
—WAYNE A. SENSOR, CEO, Alegent Health

"*Leaders Make the Future* is a must-read for those who wish to both create the future and prevail as it unfolds. With incredible clarity, Johansen articulates the new skills that future leaders *must* possess to win. I can't recommend this extraordinary book enough."
—RICK ANICETTI, President and CEO, Food Lion LLC

"In today's flat and VUCA world, among the most critical factors for effective leadership is the ability to embrace paradox, tolerate the unknown, and act flexibly. Johansen's ten leadership skills provide a highly useful guide for those who aspire to master dynamic change and create sustainably good performance."
—M. CARL JOHNSON III, Chief Strategy Officer, Campbell Soup Company

"Here you will find the leadership skills and talents that will differentiate the winners from the losers in the next decade. Using skill sets of the past to develop future capabilities is like equipping a jet to fly through the fog without the latest radar—both could lead to potential disaster."
—RAY VIGIL, Chief Learning Officer, Humana Inc.

"As leaders, we need to learn new skills to engage our associates and to influence actions for successful results. *Leaders Make the Future* gives us a practical road map for using the new leadership skills to win in the future."
—AL PLAMANN, President and CEO, Unified Grocers

"Bob Johansen is prescient in having written much of this provocative book before the economic meltdown. His advice is even more important now and jam-packed with practical gems from his own leadership experience as head of the Institute for the Future during Silicon Valley's boom, bust, and recovery."
—DAVID SIBBET, President and Founder,
The Grove Consultants International

Leaders Make the Future

Leaders Make the Future

Ten New Leadership Skills for an Uncertain World

BOB JOHANSEN

INSTITUTE FOR THE FUTURE

Berrett–Koehler Publishers, Inc.
San Francisco
a BK Business book

Berrett-Koehler Publishers, Inc.
235 Montgomery Street, Suite 650
San Francisco, CA 94104-2916
Tel: (415) 288-0260   Fax: (415) 362-2512   www.bkconnection.com

Ordering Information
Quantity sales. Special discounts are available on quantity purchases by corporations, associations, and others. For details, contact the Special Sales Department at the Berrett-Koehler address above.
Individual sales. Berrett-Koehler publications are available through most bookstores. They can also be ordered directly from Berrett-Koehler: Tel: (800) 929-2929; Fax: (802) 864-7626; www.bkconnection.com
Orders for college textbook/course adoption use. Please contact Berrett-Koehler: Tel: (800) 929-2929; Fax: (802) 864-7626.
Orders by U.S. trade bookstores and wholesalers. Please contact Ingram Publisher Services, Tel: (800) 509-4887; Fax: (800) 838-1149; E-mail: customer.service@ ingrampublisherservices.com; or visit www.ingrampublisherservices.com/ordering for details about electronic ordering.

Berrett-Koehler and the BK logo are registered trademarks of Berrett-Koehler Publishers, Inc.

Printed in the United States of America

Berrett-Koehler books are printed on long-lasting acid-free paper. When it is available, we choose paper that has been manufactured by environmentally responsible processes. These may include using trees grown in sustainable forests, incorporating recycled paper, minimizing chlorine in bleaching, or recycling the energy produced at the paper mill.

Library of Congress Cataloging-in-Publication Data

Johansen, Robert.
  Leaders make the future : ten new leadership skills for an uncertain world / Bob Johansen.
    p.   cm.
  Includes bibliographical references and index.
    ISBN 978-1-60509-002-3 (hardcover : alk. paper)   1. Leadership.   2. Executive ability. I. Title.

  HD57.7.J635   2009
  658.4'092—dc22   2009001731

First Edition

14 13 12 11 10   10 9 8 7 6 5 4 3 2

Project Management and book design: BookMatters; copyediting: Tanya Grove; proofreading: Anne Smith; indexing: Leonard Rosenbaum.

To Roy Amara

1925–2007

A leader who made the future with strength and humility

All the royalties from this book will go
to the Roy Amara Fund for Participatory Foresight,
which is an initiative to bring Roy's gift
to a much larger audience of people making the future.

Contents

Please look inside the book jacket to find the visual forecast map that provides a context of external future forces that are likely to shape leadership skills in the future.

INTRODUCTION: LEADERS NEED NEW SKILLS TO MAKE THE FUTURE

A taste of the Ten-Year Forecast map inside the book jacket, with an emphasis on external future forces that will be important for leaders to consider. • Each of the core chapters will explore a leadership skill that will be important in the future—given the external future forces of the next decade.

1 MAKER INSTINCT

Ability to exploit your inner drive to build and grow things, as well as connect with others in the making. • The maker instinct is basic to leadership in the future. • Leaders make and remake organizations.

2 CLARITY

Ability to see through messes and contradictions to a future that others cannot yet see. • Leaders are very clear about what they are making, but very flexible about how it gets made.

Ability to seed, nurture, and grow shared assets that can benefit other players—and sometimes allow competition at a higher level. · Commons creating is the ultimate future leadership skill and it benefits from all the others.

Leaders cannot predict, but they can make the future. · You can decide what kind of future you want to create and go for it. · Given the future forces of the next decade, where do you stack up in terms of your own leadership skills? · How could you improve? · This chapter will suggest ways to improve your own ability to make the future.

Figures

Preface

I study the future to learn about leadership in the present. I'm convinced that with new skills, leaders can make better organizations, better communities, and a better world.

We are entering a threshold decade: our natural, business, organizational, and social systems will reach tipping points of extreme challenge, and some of those systems are likely to break. However, such disruption can also be constructive as it can lead to new points of view—which leaders will need in order to succeed in the future world.

Self-interest will not be enough: leaders will need to broaden their concept of self to include the larger systems of which they are a part. Business leaders will still need to drive revenue, increase efficiency, and resolve conflicts, but traditional business leadership mandates won't be enough. Leaders must also embrace the shared assets and opportunities around them—not just the individual takeaways that will reward them alone.

This will be a very tough decade to be a leader, but it will also be a very exciting and meaningful time to lead, with the right set of skills and appropriate expectations.

In some sense, we all need to be our own leaders. Fortunately, the new web-based tools of leadership are making that possible right at the time when it is becoming most necessary to work together.

The more connected we are, the safer, freer, and more powerful we are—if we realize the benefits. But there are downsides: the more connected we are, the more dangerous it can be. Leaders will need to make the links and organize people for action—yet also protect against dangerous connectivity. The good news is that we are more connected than ever before, but leaders are just learning how to lead in ways that make full use of our new connectivity.

There are three overarching messages in this book:

1. The VUCA world of Volatility, Uncertainty, Complexity, and Ambiguity will get worse in the future.[1] Solvable problems will still abound, but top leaders will deal mostly with dilemmas which have no solutions, yet leaders will have to make decisions anyway. Many people are already living in a VUCA soup most of the time—especially people on the wrong side of the rich/poor gap. While I was writing this book in 2008, the VUCA world got a lot easier for me to explain. In late summer, for example, increased government regulation of Wall Street was difficult to imagine in the United States. By early fall (it felt like a matter of days), it was mandatory. That VUCA experience shook the foundations of markets around the world. Some leaders, however, are still in denial and expect a return to stability. If you are not confused by current events, however, you are not paying attention. The future can help leaders make sense of the present, but only if they learn to listen for the future. You cannot listen for the future if you are deafened by the present.

2. The VUCA world will have both danger and opportunity. Leaders will be buffeted, but they need not allow themselves to be overwhelmed, depressed, or immobilized. Some of those in authority positions today have understandably turned cranky or nasty out of frustration. Leaders must do more than *just* respond to the whirl of events, though respond they must. They can be positive change agents in the midst of chaos. Some things can get better, even as other things get worse.

3. Leaders must learn new skills in order to make a better future. Traditional leadership practices will be called into question by startling external forces and events. This book introduces ten new leadership skills for the future: maker instinct, clarity, dilemma flipping, immersive learning ability, bio-empathy, constructive depolarization, quiet transparency, smart mob organizing, and commons creating. Certainly, there will be more new skills to learn; this book seeds conversation about leadership. Cutting through chaos with these new skills, all of which will be amplified by connectivity, leaders will be able to make the future. Without them, they will be groping in the dark.

Nobody can predict the future, but you can make forecasts: plausible and internally consistent views of what might happen. A forecast is essentially a good story designed to provoke insight and invoke action. This book draws from the latest Ten-Year Forecast from Institute for the Future, which takes into account the external future forces that will shape leadership over the next decade.

I have been focused on the future since 1968, when I was a research assistant for a conference on religion and the future. I was the young guy who went to the airport to pick up the speakers, who were the world's leading futurists of the day. I listened with excitement as the future opened in front of me and the practitioners of forecasting appeared in human form.

That same year Institute for the Future (IFTF) was founded by a group of engineers and mathematicians from RAND and Stanford Research Institute (now called SRI International) as an independent nonprofit think tank. IFTF does an annual Ten-Year Forecast and has been doing so for almost forty years now. As best I can tell, it is still the only futures group that has ever outlived its forecasts—and it has done so four times over.

I was the first full-time social scientist hired at IFTF in 1973. My training was in sociology and world religions, but I've evolved into a forecaster focused on organizations, technology, and human values. In this book, I will be drawing from IFTF forecasts to set a futures context for leadership.

From 1996-2004, I was president of IFTF. During that time, the Institute boomed, almost busted, and then recovered nicely. Now I am working full time writing, speaking, and interpreting IFTF's forecasts for leaders in business, government, and nonprofit organizations.

Beginning in 2005, I wrote *Get There Early: Sensing the Future to Compete in the Present,*[2] a do-it-yourself guide to how Institute for the Future uses foresight with leaders to kindle insight and improve action. The final section of the book suggests the need for the future leadership skills that are explored in detail in *Leaders Make the Future.* These two books complement each other well.

In the spring of 2007, my colleagues Jane McGonigal and Jason Tester created a game called *Superheroes 2.0* that allowed participants to immerse themselves in the IFTF Ten-Year Forecast.[3] We played the game at our annual meeting with about 100 people. Since then, I have applied the core concepts in *Superheroes 2.0* to a wide variety of business, government, and nonprofit groups. These experiences—and Jane's and Jason's ideas in particular—have contributed greatly to the ten future leadership skills that are the core of this book.

This book was also shaped by my experience at the first Maker Faire in San Mateo—which I attended at the suggestion of my colleague David Pescovitz, one of the original contributors to *MAKE: Magazine.* It was a gathering of wonderful and eccentric people who built things that staggered my imagination. Three years later, IFTF organized a booth at the Maker Faire, with the goal of helping participants make sense out of its complex reality. That weekend it drew 70,000 people who liked to build and share what they had built.

At Institute for the Future, an event or happening in the present that gives indication of a future direction is called a "signal." Maker Faire is a signal that the ancient do-it-yourself instinct is being reborn into something much bigger, transforming solo leadership into more of a do-it-ourselves leadership.[4]

All humans have at least a touch of what I call the maker instinct, but most leaders have a serious dose since they must make and remake the organizations they lead. The best leaders have always been tinkerers who imagine alternative structures and love to play around with them to see what new things they can create. Now, with amazing new tools and network connectivity, profoundly different organizations can be built.

This is my eighth book, but writing this one was very different from my previous experiences as an author. My other books seemed to be running away from me as I wrote them, and I had to struggle to catch them. This one came at me so fast I could not avoid it. Daily events fed right into the book—it just wanted to be written. I have a very personal urge to share what I've learned about leadership and the future.

This book is not an Institute for the Future consensus view of leadership. I do not presume to speak for my colleagues on this important topic, for they have rich experiences of their own. I have, however, been shaped by my experiences at IFTF and the many diverse organizations with whom we work.

My goal is to help leaders make the future a better place in which to live. This book shares what I've learned about leadership, as well as my advice for future leaders, given the future external forces. I hope you will improve your own readiness for the future by learning the skills in this book and by developing new skills beyond the ten that I've imagined. You do not have to believe in the value of the skills in this book to find them useful. In fact, they may be most useful if they provoke you to imagine your own future leadership skills.

Over my long career at IFTF, I have seen big shifts in leadership—including my own. We are all on the brink of further shifts that will be even more dramatic than what we have experienced to date. The future forces of the next decade will be extremely challenging for leaders of all kinds.

The space between judging too soon (the classic mistake of problem solvers) and deciding too late (the classic mistake of academics) is a space leaders of the future must love—without staying there too long. Leaders need to reflect on the future, but they must also make decisions in the present.

Bob Johansen
Palo Alto, California
2009

INTRODUCTION

Leaders Need New Skills to Make the Future

If a man take no thought of what is distant,
he will find sorrow near at hand.

CONFUCIUS

LEADERS MUST LEARN how to make the future in the midst of volatility, uncertainty, complexity, and ambiguity. The discipline of foresight can help leaders make better decisions today. We need not passively accept the future. Leaders can and must *make* a better future. That is what this book is all about.

It is hard to even think about the future if you are overwhelmed by the present, yet that is exactly the time when foresight can be most practical. A global futures perspective can help leaders make sense out of the chaotic patterns of change in the external world. Looking to distant possibilities can provide new insight for the present.

Leaders are already experiencing volatility, uncertainty, complexity, and ambiguity (VUCA), but many of their responses are not constructive and the prospects for leadership in the future are not secure. Some leaders will judge too soon and draw simplistic conclusions while others will decide too late and pay a price for their lack of courage or inaction. Some will be overwhelmed by a sense of help-

1

lessness while others will become cynical and question everything around them. Some will react with anger. Some will pick a side and start to fight. And some leaders will deny the crisis or truly believe that the chaos will just go away. Such leadership responses are both understandable and dysfunctional.

Leaders need not be overwhelmed and pummeled by the world of VUCA. The future will also be loaded with opportunities. Leaders must have the skills to take advantage of those opportunities, as well as the agility to sidestep the dangers.

This book will unfold the ten new leadership skills in a definite order, moving from instinctual to complex. Each of the ten core chapters will describe a future leadership skill that any leader can either develop personally or partner with someone else to perform. The core chapters will help leaders answer these questions:

Chapter 1: How can you draw out your inner *maker instinct* and apply it to your leadership? Future leaders will need both a can-do and a can-make spirit.

Chapter 2: How can you, as a leader, create and communicate with *clarity* in confusing times—without being simplistic?

Chapter 3: How can you improve your skills at *dilemma flipping* so that you succeed with challenges that cannot be solved and won't go away?

Chapter 4: Do you have an *immersive learning ability* so that you can learn by immersing yourself in new physical and virtual worlds that may be uncomfortable for you?

Chapter 5: Do you have *bio-empathy* to learn from nature and use that wisdom to inform your decisions?

Chapter 6: Can you *constructively depolarize* conflict to both calm and improve the situation?

Chapter 7: Do you lead with a *quiet transparency* so you are open but not self-promoting?

Chapter 8: Can you do *rapid prototyping* by working through many scenarios during the process of development?

Chapter 9: Can you *organize smart mobs* using a range of media?

Chapter 10: Can you *create commons* within which both cooperation and competition may occur?

Our ways of thinking about the future have evolved fundamentally over the years. This artifact from the past comes from the 1964 World's Fair Futurama pavilion sponsored by General Motors. (See Figure 1.)

FIGURE 1. Badge from 1964 World's Fair Futurama pavilion sponsored by General Motors. *Source:* IFTF personal GM artifact, 2008.

Made of lightweight metal and designed so that it could be attached to your pocket or shirt, this motto reveals the popular view of the future in 1964. In those days, the future was something that could only be envisioned by a large company such as General Motors. The future was distant and driven by technology. Today, would most consumers trust GM—or any other large corporation for that matter—to create the future? I think not.

In 1964, the future was perceived as something so complicated that everyday people could only glimpse it if the big companies, powerful government agencies, or scientists gave them that chance. Leaders in this world were not very accessible—nor was the future they were thought to be creating.

In 2008, after discovering this vision of the future from the past, Jason Tester, who designs artifacts from the future at IFTF, remade a new artifact based on the slogan "I have seen the future," but injected it with modern maker spirit. (See Figure 2.)

FIGURE 2. New version of an old slogan. *Source:* IFTF, *The Future of Making,* 2008. SR# 1154.

This artifact captures the spirit of 2009 looking ahead to 2019 and beyond. Big companies, government agencies, or universities will not create the future, although they can certainly affect it. People will make the future, working together. "I am making the future" is a call to action, with an attitude.

The maker instinct is the most basic future leadership skill, and it energizes every other skill. All ten of the future leadership skills proposed in this book build on each other and work together. Clarity, for example, wraps a leader's vision in practical but inspirational language that motivates people through chaos. Creating commons is the most ambitious and demanding new leadership skill. Every leadership skill is present in every other skill, and leaders need to decide which skills to emphasize when.

On the map inside the book jacket is a summary of the external future forces around us that will shape all ten of the future leadership skills. Each chapter uses these forces as lenses through which to view a particular leadership skill.

Leadership must change because of the external future forces. The global rich/poor gap is the most basic and the most extreme future force. People who are poor already experience the VUCA world: their lives are volatile, uncertain, complex, and ambiguous every day. Realistically and sadly, it is hard to forecast a narrowing of this gap, but easy to imagine it getting wider.

In *Get There Early*, I wrote an entire chapter on "The VUCA World: Danger and Opportunity."[1] VUCA is not new. There has been plenty of volatility, uncertainty, complexity, and ambiguity for leaders to deal with (or not) in the past. The need for leadership in the face of uncertainty is also not new. What will be new in the years ahead is the scale and intensity of the likely disruptions. Having spent forty years forecasting, I believe that the future world will be *more* volatile, *more* uncertain, *more* complex, and *more* ambiguous, or so it will seem if you are in a seat of leadership.

In forty years of IFTF forecasting, the direst forecasts yet are in *Get There Early* and *Leaders Make the Future*. As frightening as they are, however, they can also be motivational. Many people, I hope, will dedicate themselves to proving us forecasters wrong.

One of my jobs as a forecaster is to help people learn how to be comfortable being uncomfortable—but certainly not passively comfortable. The most important value of forecasting is to help people learn to lead aggressively even if they feel uneasy. Discomfort will come with the territory for the next ten years—and probably far beyond. Leaders must not only get used to it, but learn to like it. If you are lucky enough to experience a future that is less chaotic, take it as a blessing and be happy that you are prepared for surprises, since you are still likely to experience them later in life. For most leaders, few things are predictable or slow moving.

Figure 3 summarizes the Foresight to Insight to Action Cycle that is described in detail in *Get There Early*. Even if you don't agree with a forecast, it can be very useful to provoke insight. The purpose of forecasting is not to predict the future—nobody can do that—but to make better decisions in the present. The ten new leadership skills that are the core of this book summarize my forecast: they are plausible, internally consistent, and provocative statements about what will be most important for leaders in the years ahead. They are intended to encourage you to consider what leadership skills you will need to succeed—given the external future forces of the next decade. As a forecaster, I can provide you with foresight, but it is up to you to come up with the insight and act upon it.

Notice the positive definition of VUCA inside the Foresight to

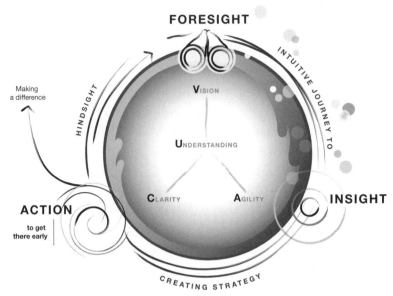

FIGURE 3. The Foresight → Insight → Action Cycle. See *Get There Early* for more detail. *Source:* IFTF, 2007. SR# 1038.

Insight to Action Cycle. Leaders in the future will need to have Vision, Understanding, Clarity, and Agility. The negative VUCA can be turned around with effective leadership that follows these principles:

- Volatility yields to vision.
- Uncertainty yields to understanding.
- Complexity yields to clarity.
- Ambiguity yields to agility.

The VUCA world of the future will be formidable and loaded with opportunities. The biggest danger is not being prepared—and you can control that by preparing yourself and your organization. The best way to be prepared is to look ten years ahead.

Ten Years Ahead: The Magic Time Frame

Making the future begins with understanding the future. Foresight can help you do that, even though the future is unpredictable. At Institute for the Future, we've found that the sweet spot for forecasting is about ten years ahead. Ten years is far enough in the future to be beyond the planning horizon of most organizations, yet it is not so far out that it seems unbelievable or irrelevant. Ten years is also far enough ahead to see clear patterns that are not visible in the noise of the present. Foresight helps you discern what is important in the long run. If you understand the external future forces, you can figure out the leadership skills that are likely to be needed.

Starting from the Institute for the Future's Ten-Year Forecasts, this book looks ahead to explore the leadership skills necessary to succeed in the future. Inside this book jacket is a map which summarizes our Ten-Year Forecast of external future forces. This introduction gives a quick tour of its key elements.

Each chapter is organized around a future leadership skill, beginning with basic orientation and grounding. Then links are made between the IFTF Ten-Year Forecast and that particular skill. Each of the ten future leadership skills corresponds to an iconic image intended to evoke a particular feeling, drawn by artist and documentary filmmaker Anthony Weeks who has worked with me for years to visualize the futures that we discuss in workshops.

When you take off the book jacket, notice the look and feel of the map. It is an organic matrix—a kind of conundrum itself—which aptly represents the forecast for the next ten years in that we are moving into a world in which changes will unfold organically and also threaten nature. Engineering and mechanical thinking drove the last economic era; the next era will be driven by biology and the life sciences. On the map, the language is linked to nature in underlying metaphors and background graphics.

The book jacket forecast map summarizes these external future forces that will be important for future leaders to consider. To the right of the map, you see the ten leadership abilities that are most important for this future world. The ten chapters that follow describe each of those skills, along with the abilities, competencies, and traits that will fit together to create a new leadership profile for the future. The book concludes with personal guidelines for future leaders, with a focus on what you can do to be more prepared for the future you intend to make.

At the center of the forecast for the next decade is the gap between rich and poor and the cascading injustices that result from extreme imbalances of wealth. For much of the developing world, hunger, safety, and subsistence are still daily challenges. Meanwhile, the much smaller so-called developed world population consumes proportionately many more resources. In the future, a variety of new media will make the rich/poor gap even more visible than it is today—from both sides. The world has always had a rich/poor gap, but it is likely to get larger and it certainly will become more visible and have impacts on all portions of the map.

The columns on the map are the most important drivers, or future forces, that leaders should consider:

Diasporas: New Emerging Economies. "Diaspora" is a very old word that refers to the Jews who were separated from the Promised Land. These were people linked to a specific land but were also a people "set apart." The concept of a diaspora is particularly familiar to people who are Jewish or African American, or anyone who has studied the Old Testament. Diaspora is also a very useful concept for understanding the future.

Future diasporas will be different. They will be less linked to geography, but more linked virtually. Some will still retain deep historical traditions, but others will be more modern. Many kinds of diasporas will be important, including these:

- Climate change diasporas, displaced by weather disruptions and linked by a common tragedy, like the Hurricane Katrina diaspora.

- Rural-to-urban diasporas will be common over the next decade, as we shift from being a primarily rural planet to a primarily urban one. Rural-to-urban diasporas are likely to be most dramatic in China, India, and Africa. Many, including children, will be left behind.

- Cultural diasporas, such as offshore Chinese or Indians in the technology industry in Silicon Valley and other parts of the world. Of course, both China and India are so large that there are many different subsets of these diasporas.

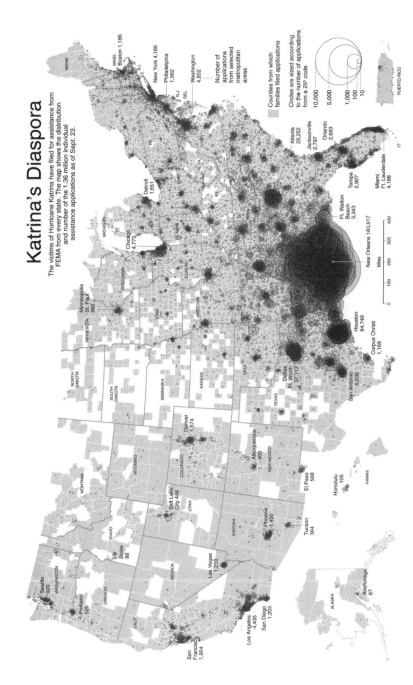

Katrina's Diaspora

The victims of Hurricane Katrina have filed for assistance from FEMA from every state. The map shows the distribution and number of the 1.36 million individual assistance applications as of Sept. 23.

Boston 1,186
New York 4,186
Philadelphia 1,562
Washington 4,852
Atlanta 29,252
Jacksonville 2,797
Orlando 2,693
Tampa 2,907
Miami Ft. Lauderdale 4,188
Ft. Walton Beach 3,343
New Orleans 183,617
Detroit 1,651
Chicago 4,773
Minneapolis St. Paul 969
Houston 84,749
Corpus Christi 1,169
Dallas Ft. Worth 37,113
San Antonio 6,035
Denver 1,574
Albuquerque 405
El Paso 568
Tucson 364
Phoenix 1,400
Salt Lake City 448
Boise 88
Las Vegas 1,210
Los Angeles 4,435
San Diego 1,203
San Francisco 1,954
Seattle 920
Portland 520
Honolulu 105
Anchorage 67

Number of applications from selected metropolitan areas

Counties from which families filed applications

Circles are sized according to the number of applications from a ZIP code

10,000
5,000
1,000
100
10

Miles
0 100 200 300 400

PUERTO RICO

FIGURE 4. This map shows the distribution of applications for assistance filed by displaced victims of Hurricane Katrina.[2]

Source: Used with permission of *New York Times* Graphics, © 2005.

- Corporate diasporas, such as alumni of McKinsey, IBM, or Apple. Companies that abide by the maxim "we're in it for the long run" include both current and former employees—as well as close friends of the family, suppliers, contractors, and others.

- Bio-diasporas, which share biological traits, health conditions, or biometric markers in common. People with similar disease states, for example, form very strong support groups and are very effective users of the Internet, through sites such as www.patientslikeme.com.

- Financial diasporas, such as the Islamic financial communities that are creating new kinds of mortgages, bonds, insurance, and even currencies within the belief system or theology of the Islamic faith. Islamic finance is not new, but the Western world knew little about it until recently.

Diasporas can be good, but they can also be evil. Think of them as networks of people who may be physically separated but are bound tightly by shared values. In our forecasts at IFTF, we consider diasporas as more important than traditional governmental or regional links in emerging economies. Indeed, in many parts of the developing world, diasporas are thoroughly integrated into both government and business practices. Within diasporas, innovations and ideas spread much more quickly because of common beliefs and high trust.

Diasporas often have a strong insider/outsider dynamic; members in one have a common bond. It can take longer for people on the outside—sometimes much longer—to build trust and a working relationship with diaspora members. Leaders must understand diasporas and be able to engage with them. In fact, most leaders themselves belong to at least one. What diasporas define who you are? Which ones can you easily identify? Which ones could amplify your leadership and which ones threaten you or your vision of the future?

Civil Society: What Will We Choose to Do Together?[3] There are many different ways to mix business, government, nonprofit, and community interests all over the globe. On my first morning in China I vividly remember a newspaper article that referred casually to the "socialist market economy." That phrase popped off the page as I read it. Like many Americans, I had thought of economies as being either socialist *or* market–driven. In China, the economy is both, mixing government and markets in ways that bewilder outsiders and sometimes even the Chinese people. What is the role of government? What is the role of markets? What roles do communities and individual people play?

Governments, markets, and people will interact in complex ways in the future—and many of those interactions will be through electronic connectivity. Networked connectivity can help to pull things together, and there will be many new opportunities to improve our civic infrastructure and our ability to cooperate. We are more connected than ever, but that does not mean we are automatically cohesive. The potential of connectivity, however, is extremely powerful. The more connected we are, the better we can work together—for broader benefit. The more connected we are, the more quickly disruptions can spread—as they did with global credit markets in 2008. Leaders in the future will have new opportunities to engage with the society around them using new infrastructures for cooperation. Competition and cooperation will need to coexist in ways that will vary from region to region, country to country, and even at times from city to city.

Corporations will play a major role in shaping the future. Although separate from government, there will be many ways in which they will need to work together. Corporations are often more technologically advanced and faster to change than governments. Still, we need at least some common infrastructure and shared services to succeed. Deciding what we choose to do together and what we leave to the marketplace will be key decisions for leaders in the future.

Food: The Flashpoint for Rich/Poor Conflict. Food is basic to life and the next decade will be a critical period for food production and distribution. Global climate change is an underlying shift with deep implications, but there are many more interacting variables to consider. Food is not just functional; it is deeply cultural. Over the next decade, food will be scarce in many parts of the world, and food safety will be a continuing challenge for all. Without healthy food, little else matters.

Distribution of food will be just as important as producing it. People are spread out and food must get to them. Where food comes from is becoming an important part of how it is valued. Food from some places may not be safe, or at least may not be perceived as safe. Food—and specifically the shortage of food—will be a flashpoint for conflicts, which will often be between rich and poor.

Ecosystems: Navigation of Life. The lack of response to global climate change aptly demonstrates the short-sightedness of our government and businesses that do not take into account the larger context of life. In the world of today, profit is measured by narrow economic criteria like quarterly returns. Profitability over time will take place in the larger context of sustainability. Global climate change is a wake-up call: it is important to think not only years ahead but generations ahead. Natural ecosystems are both robust and fragile.

Global climate change will shadow the next decade and beyond. Most climate models suggest that the majority of serious negative effects will happen beyond ten years from now, but the decisions we make in the next decade will have long-term impacts. Ten years may seem long to most companies and government agencies, but it is a short time in the context of climate cycles. Leaders will need to think about these larger ecosystem issues as an important part of every-day decisions. Humans are having profound impacts on the earth. Leaders in the next decade will not just be leading organizations; they will be leading life. Leaders have a chance to make the world at least a bit more sustainable.

Amplified Individuals: Extending the Human Body. In the next decade, there is real potential for many people to be better than normal, healthier, higher-performing, and live longer than ever before. Of course, there is also a health gap that mirrors the rich/poor gap. While many will struggle to live at all, others will be healthier than normal and a few may enjoy much longer life spans. Minds, bodies, and networks will all be connected in novel and powerful ways to create extended individuals who are amplified in ways we can only begin to imagine. Leaders will control new tools of human amplification, but individuals who may not have the same agenda or values will challenge them.

The Baby Boom generation will lead the way in body extensions as they wrestle with the process of their own aging. This is the generation of people who said when they were young: "Don't trust anyone over thirty." As they age, I expect one of their leaders will coin a new generational motto: "Don't trust anyone under sixty." The Boomers will want to extend their lives and experiment with life—as they have at each stage as they have aged. The Boomers will have a new medical tool kit with which to experiment.

Amplified individuals will create amplified organizations. Our global connectivity is growing dramatically, which is creating new ways to organize ourselves. Think of a leader not just as an individual but as a node on many different networks. The best leaders are not isolated; they are ravenous networkers with active links all around the world. In the future, economies of scale (in which bigger is almost always better) give way to economies of organization (in which you are what you can organize). Leadership is all about engagement, and networked media provide several ways in which leaders can engage to make better futures. The most connected leaders will be the best leaders.

These external forces will appear in each of the next ten chapters that focus on leadership skills for the future. They provide a context for assessing what skills will be most important. Although the rest of the book focuses on the future, it is important to start with a touch of what history has taught us about leadership already.

Enduring Leadership Skills

When we do ten-year forecasting at IFTF, we always look back as well as forward. Most things that happen are not really new. Often those things we think of as "new" were tried and failed years ago. At IFTF, we used to say that we look back at least twice as far as we look ahead. Now we feel that going back even further is necessary. I recommend studying the previous thirty to fifty years as part of every ten-year forecasting effort. For a recent forecast on green health, Rod Falcon and his Health Horizons team at IFTF actually looked two hundred years back as well as ten years ahead. This is the largest time span I have ever seen in a forecast and it was completely appropriate—given the long history of linking nature and health.

Each of the ten future leadership skills has roots in the past. As novelist William Gibson said, "The future is already here—it's just unevenly distributed."[4] Some of these skills are visible in today's leaders; and some of them have been used successfully in the past, but they will be much more important in the future.

When I became president of IFTF in 1996, I began a list of principles to guide me as a leader. I had studied leadership but had not been a leader myself on this scale. Being the president was much tougher than I expected. I realize now that many of the challenges were inside my head. I was frequently frustrated and occasionally downright discouraged. I had physical reactions, such as headaches, almost every afternoon. I had emotional reactions, such as unexpected tears. These symptoms convinced me that I needed to make changes in how I was living and how I was leading. This eight-year immersion experience taught me that being a leader is much harder than studying leadership. Being president during a very difficult time gave me first-hand experience that I can now share in this book. I've also been influenced greatly by the wide range of leaders with whom I have worked.

This book focuses on the new leadership, but not everything about leaders in the future will be new. Some leadership traits will continue to be important, although in updated forms. Here are some enduring leadership skills that I admire greatly:

Physical and Mental Discipline: The ability to inspire people in a gripping way with physical and spiritual energy. In my experience, physical exercise and healthy living are vital to leadership. More information is available to those who want to lead a healthy lifestyle, but it takes personal discipline as well. Leaders must develop physical and emotional energies that work for them as individuals as well as inspire those around them. Leaders need to be coaches for others, but also need to be their own guides. For example, Marge Kiley coaches gymnastics, a sport in which a mistake could mean death. I asked her what mental discipline she teaches. She said it depends: If the young-ster is a risk taker, she teaches the discipline of watching themselves while performing so they can see how difficult and dangerous moves can be. On the other hand, with students who are overly cautious, she tells them to concentrate on what it feels like to perform from inside their heads. Essentially, this is the ancient tension between leading and watching yourself lead.

Active Attention: The ability to filter out noise and distraction, combined with a strong ability to stay centered—even when overwhelmed with stimuli. No leader could absorb everything, even in the old days before the Internet. All leaders must filter and learn how to see patterns as they emerge. The difficulty in screening dramatically increases as data sources multiply. Generational differences will become more apparent in the future, especially as young "digital natives" who learned to use media at an early age and have better skills for "continuous partial attention"[5] move into leadership roles. Filtering has always been important for leaders, but in the data-everywhere world of tomorrow it will be extremely challenging.

Readiness Discipline: The abilities to anticipate, prepare, and practice. You cannot control the VUCA world, but you can be more or less ready for unexpected events. Leadership has always benefitted from preparedness, but the demand for it will be much greater in a world of increasing uncertainty. Surprises are inevitable. Leaders can, however, consider a wide range of alternative scenarios and practice how they might respond. Readiness discipline will be explored in more detail in chapter 4 on Immersive Learning Ability. Leaders cannot predict but they can prepare.

Urgent Patience: Ability to judge when to add new challenges and when to counsel steady persistence. Bill Walsh, who coached the San Francisco 49ers when they were a great team, saw this as a key leadership trait: to discern when people are overloaded (and be patient with them in those times) and when they are overly confident (and press them with appropriate urgency). Leaders can be both urgent and patient, depending on what is needed at the time. The role of a leader, he said, was to listen for and apply this strategy he called "urgent patience."

Story Telling and Listening: Ability to discover and tell engaging stories that help people form a particular vision of the future. Great leaders are usually great storytellers. While problems can be summarized in a formula or an algorithm, it takes a story to understand a dilemma. The future will be loaded with dilemmas, so it will take lots of stories to help make sense out of them. Many of these will be mysteries and some will be thrillers and they will be told by leaders through a dizzying array of media.

Humble Strength: Ability to act with courage and clear intent, in an authentic, engaging, and self-effacing way. This leadership skill will be more difficult to achieve in a fragmented multimedia world. Thinking about the long-term future certainly breeds humility. This enduring strength will be explored in more detail in chapter 7 on Quiet Transparency.

Synchronicity: Ability to make meaning from new stimuli by finding connections and patterns that are not obvious to others. Leaders need to see patterns before others see them. The ability to see links between personal experience and future possibilities will be essential. Great leaders have always had this ability, but in the future the patterns are likely to be more difficult to discern.

In addition to these enduring abilities, leaders will need to change in dramatic ways, which in turn will create a demand for new leadership skills. *Leaders Make the Future* is structured around ten new leadership skills necessary to respond to external future forces. I struggled with what to call these characteristics of leadership. Skills? Competencies? Abilities? Traits? Styles? I decided to call them skills—since I am convinced that they can be learned—and I want to emphasize those areas where leaders can improve themselves.

All leaders have innate personal skills that they should leverage, but there is much more for all of us to learn. This book is about changes in how leaders will need to lead. Leaders will make the future, but not by themselves and not without new skills.

1

Maker Instinct

Ability to exploit your inner drive to build and grow things,
as well as connect with others in the making.

EVERYONE HAS SOME MAKER INSTINCT. The challenge is to turn the natural urge to create into a leadership skill, to synchronize the maker instincts of leaders with those of others. Many people don't realize their own maker instinct and potential. It must be recognized, valued, and nurtured if it is to become a leadership skill for the future. Beyond do-it-yourself, we need to nurture *do-it-ourselves* leadership. The maker instinct will be amplified by connectivity.

When I go into a new company, I like to ask leaders about their hobbies. If they have complex, exotic, time-consuming hobbies, it may be that their maker instinct is not being fully expressed at work. Perhaps the organization is operating at a routine level that does not demand deep engagement and does not tap the maker instinct of its leaders.

I remember meeting one executive who rebuilt old steam engines in his spare time. Building steam engines is a great hobby, but this top executive was overdosing: he had fields packed with steam engines. As I learned more about his company and his role, I realized that the corporate culture did not tap into the maker instinct. Rather, the leaders in that company tended to do what they had to do at work, then go home to do what they wanted to do. They had created a culture of discipline focused on good management, but they were not tapping the maker instinct and channeling it into leadership.

I'm certainly not against hobbies, but I am against leadership roles that focus on bottom line results, telling people what to do, and following the rules, rather than requiring leaders to get personally involved in *how* things work and how they could be improved. For example, some people like to arrive, give a speech, and leave. They have no interest in the group process that was unfolding before they arrived and will continue after they depart. On the other hand, makers *like* to see how ideas develop and unfold—and they like to be able to influence how that happens. Leaders need to get involved in the messiness of group process to understand the context for decision making and the underlying relationships among the people working together. The speak-and-run approach may be considered leadership on the speaking circuit, but that's not group leadership. Leaders have the maker (and remaker) instinct to engage in the process, to figure out how things work and what needs to change.

The maker instinct is basic and precedes all other skills that will be needed for future leadership. The roots of the maker instinct run deep. Go to any beach in the world and you see kids digging in the sand. Why do they dig holes and build sand castles? These young makers are honing their maker instinct. My guess is that most successful leaders were very ambitious excavators when they were kids. Leaders are makers by definition. They make organizations, with more or less involvement by others.

The leaders of the future will be less controlling, since there will be fewer things they can control. They will also be more engaged with others, since connectivity will be required to make the future. Everyone is part of a network. Leaders are nodes, and the best ones are hubs that form, nurture, and grow networks that stretch far beyond the individual leader.

My dad was a maker. To relax, he would go to the basement by himself, where he always had several projects in progress. With great care, he read *Popular Mechanics*, a magazine that aroused the maker instinct in readers every month with inspiring projects like gliders you could pull behind a car. Dad had a Shopsmith woodworking machine—a noisy, whirring contraption that loomed near our furnace. I learned as a child that this awe-inspiring machine was dangerous and that I should stay away unless I myself learned how to become a maker. It was not easy to learn woodworking skills, and I never became nearly as good as my dad, but I still have a serving tray that I made at a Cub Scout meeting using discarded records from a local radio station and imprinting circular patterns on them with a spinning wire brush. My dad made it easy for me to satisfy my early urge to make, giving me lots of advice while he watched over me so I didn't get hurt. The Shopsmith was frighteningly mechanical, but it was also a wonder. Like the maker instinct itself, it was both attractive and imposing.

My dad was a solo maker, working alone in our basement. In the future, solo makers will still be around, but networks of makers will be much more powerful. The maker instinct is solitary, but leaders will need to connect their maker energy to others in order to fuel change. Makers have always been interested in sharing what they make with others and the new media tools will facilitate this urge.

My mom had the maker instinct as well. She loved to sew and then to knit. She made clothes for my sister and me, though I didn't appreciate them until I got older. At our church, my mom and grandmother would go to sewing circles where people would talk as they sewed or knitted. Late in her life, my grandmother became part of the Leisure League at church, a group that made clothing for people in developing countries. She loved the making, but the fact that others valued her products and found them useful gave them meaning. That work became a big part of my grandmother's identity. Everyone has a maker instinct, but it can play out in many different ways with different people. The maker instinct is both male and female and is found across cultures as well.

MAKE: Magazine is a modern reinvention of *Popular Mechanics* and the other maker magazines of that era. Its founder, Dale Dougherty, is well aware of the historical roots of his magazine and what he refers to as the "maker mindset." In honor of those roots, *MAKE* is exactly the same size in its paper version as *Popular Mechanics, Popular Science,* and the other do-it-yourself magazines that were popular thirty years ago. Makers tend to respect their roots, and many makers have deep roots.

Maker instinct is a kind of DNA imprint that we all carry in our own ways. *MAKE: Magazine* and the Maker Faire are profound signals that indicate a very important direction for the future. The maker instinct is a drive away from the ordinary—including ordinary leadership.

Maker Instinct Defined

The maker instinct is an inner drive to build and grow things. Leaders with maker instinct have a constant desire to improve the organizations around them. Both managers and leaders ask how things work, but leaders have an urge to make them work *better.*

For example, when I was a Little League Baseball manager for my son's team, my maker instinct urged me to juggle the lineup to try out different batting orders for maximum effect. When I was president of Institute for the Future, I was fascinated by how organizational changes might better achieve our mission. The popular Kevin Costner movie *Field of Dreams* is a romantic fantasy around a maker theme: "If you build it, they will come." He made a baseball field in the middle of an Iowa cornfield and a miracle happened. True, the Costner character was a bit idealistic and even unrealistic, but he also had an overwhelming maker urge that just had to be expressed. He was right to follow that urge.

Makers like to be hands-on and see things from the inside. The *MAKE: Magazine* motto is "if you can't open it, you don't own it." Open means transparent and accessible, but it also means able to be altered, customized, or personalized. Think about how that maxim has major implications for today's manufacturers, many of whom do not want you to open their products and will void your warranty if you do. Of course, the specifics of how consumers are allowed to "open" a product are critical. The Toyota Scion, for example, is designed to be customized, but that doesn't mean that everything about the Scion is open. Manufacturers must decide what they can "open," while still owning what they can own that gives them advantage. This is not an either/or choice. The clear direction of change, however, is toward being more open and more willing to let consumers engage with and modify the products they buy.

Leaders will grow, re-grow, and reimagine their own organizations again and again. The maker instinct fuels that growth. Leaders will make the future in the context of the external future forces of the next decade.

Maker Instinct Meets the Future

In the future, personal empowerment will mean that customization and personalization will be desired and often demanded. Even global products will need to feel local, or at least not feel foreign. Grassroots economic systems like eBay will make bottom-up financial transactions possible. Smart networking will create results that will not be predicted but will be profound.

DIASPORAS OF MAKERS WILL GROW

At the 2008 Maker Faire, IFTF gave visitors inexpensive video recorders and asked them to go out and gather stories from the makers. They brought back accounts of the maker instinct at work. For example, a twenty-foot-high electric giraffe named Russell created quite a stir rolling around the fair. Russell cost its maker $20,000 plus lots of time to build it. Colorful cupcakes, each one accommodating a

FIGURE 5. Poster for Maker Faire.[1] *Source:* Used with permission of O'Reilly Media, Inc.

single rider, rolled around the grounds in wandering paths. The two liquid sculptors dropped Mentos candies into Diet Coke bottles to create patterns of spray.

Computer giant and master maker Steve Wozniak spoke at the second Maker Faire and commented that the spirit of Maker Faire reminded him of the early days of the personal computer. Many of today's makers are out to create new products or services, but others are just out to have a good time. Makers are coming together in new ways that are likely to have profound impacts on the future.

Maker communities, as showcased at the Maker Faire, are often diasporas linked by strong shared values and sometimes a common place where its members feel at home. Many of these communities are bound together by ideals about how their work should be practiced, or where their craft was born. Maker diasporas believe in what they are making and how it is made. They often want to spread their word and share their truth. The annual Maker Faire is a vibrant gathering of makers shouting out to a wide array of other makers and celebrants of all ages. Although showing off is part of it, far more is going on.

There is often a strong bond among makers that stretches back in time and forward. Leaders share stories that keep maker traditions alive and draw in new members. Makers have the skills to make the world a better place, but they often don't know it. They just build what gives them pleasure, but leaders will know how to tap that maker energy as a force for change.

Shared energy is what diasporas are all about. The maker instinct will feed right into diasporic energy which will be amplified by networked media. As these new groundswells of grassroots innovation disrupt traditional patterns, however, organizations are likely to be confused about what to do. For example, both Mentos and Coca-Cola threatened to sue the artists whom they claimed were misusing their products by dropping Mentos into Diet Coke and creating massive displays of fizz. A short while later, both companies realized that lawsuits were unlikely to be successful and were likely to be unpopular with consumers. With some consternation but great consumer insight, both companies decided to sponsor the artists. Makers learn from those who use their products and services, and they learn even more when they encourage people to use them in ways that the manufacturer never imagined.

Solo makers like my dad in his basement are evolving into networked artisans through gatherings like the Maker Faire. Makers love to show and tell. The website Instructables.com allows makers to meet virtually and share projects. The banner on the Instructables home page even refers to itself as "The World's Largest Show and Tell."[2] Maker messages will circulate very rapidly within and among maker diasporas. Products will be turned into stories and the stories will spread like viruses on maker blogs and every other imaginable medium.

MAKERS WILL CREATE SHARED SPACES

One leadership dilemma is how to intelligently give things away without putting your own organization at a disadvantage. Remember: your competitors don't necessarily need to lose in order for you to win. Open source logic teaches that it can be good to give away ideas if there is a good chance that you will get back even better ideas in return. This logic is counterintuitive for many leaders, but those who tap into the maker instinct understand this concept much more readily than those whose maker instincts were repressed in large corporations. Makers easily access the wisdom they have learned from their hobbies to help them with the demands of their jobs.

At the 2008 Maker Faire, for example, Jimmy Smith from Team FredNet talked about the Google Lunar X Prize, which was awarded to the team that could land a rover on the surface of the moon. FredNet used only off-the-shelf products. They shared their activities with everyone, including their competitors. Thus a new zone was created within which competitors could pool their resources in order to achieve the ultra-ambitious goal of landing a rover on the moon. This logic challenges traditional assumptions about competition. You divulge information to competitors? Yes, in pursuit of the prize there is sharing, but competition continues beyond that base of information.

Corporations used to think of research and development (R&D) as something that happens inside big laboratories and gradually gets released to the people who use the products. In the future, much of the innovation will come from backyards, basements, and kitchens of those guided by their own maker instinct—in both developed and (especially) developing worlds. At the edges of traditional R&D— and even far beyond the edges—corporate-mandated methods are giving way to maker-inspired grassroots innovation. Central corporate R&D will still exist, but it will be more open and on a smaller scale. Threadless, for example, is a T-shirt maker that holds a design competition in which consumers compete and vote on the designs. Those that get the highest ratings get manufactured. The Threadless model may be extreme, but it suggests the direction of change. End consumers can be the designers—or at least the inspiration—for future products.

MAKERS AND THE TOOLS OF WARFARE

When I started out as a forecaster in the early 1970s, many leading-edge information technologies were developed within the Advanced Research Projects Agency (ARPA), which created the ARPAnet, the precursor to the Internet. Gradually, innovations that were classified as military secrets made their way to public use. In just the thirty-five-year period of my career, this pattern has reversed. Now, the leading-edge tools are coming from consumer electronics and video gaming. Even the tools of war are coming from everyday products adapted with a mix of maker ingenuity and anger. The most sophisticated roadside bombs used in insurgent warfare, for example, come from consumer electronic and cell phone technologies—not from sophisticated big-technology innovation developed inside massive defense establishments. Insurgent makers are everywhere—on the battlefield and behind the scenes. Gradually, these innovations make their way back to the military industrial complex.

Innovation will have both positive and negative results. In a world of asymmetric warfare, innovation happens from the bottom up. Enemies (and potential collaborators) can come together any place and any time. Terrorist networks tend to be organizationally sophisticated, and they know how to make their own weapons. The maker instinct is often very strong within dangerous mobs, and it is likely to grow in the future. Access to tools has improved for the bad guys as well as for the good guys, and sometimes it will be difficult to tell which is which. Makers, alas, can be thieves or vandals, demonstrating the negative side—even as the positive energy of events like the Maker Faire continues to grow.

MAKERS IN THE MARKETPLACE

Global climate change and an ecosystem that is clearly at risk will continue to be concerns in the next decade. Meanwhile, a new generation of makers is coming of age. Stimulated by the first round of ecological thinking in the late '60s and early '70s, schools provided students with a strong dose of environmental education. These next generation makers are more likely to be eco-motivated and guided by a new mantra to reduce, reuse, and *remake*. Remaking will be even more important for this new generation of eco-makers than making. Their exchanges will grow into marketplaces for goods and services.

Etsy.com, for example, is an online marketplace for makers to buy and sell. Swapthing.com is a sort of eBay for people who want to trade rather than buy. Both Etsy and Swapthing are indicative of this new generation of makers who want to reuse more and consume less. They salvage what they can and redesign existing products for new applications. Green aspirations will translate into a bottom-up economy of makers who are skeptical about big corporations and planned obsolescence. Maker gatherings already tend to be green, and they are likely to get much greener in the future. People want green energy, and corporations are made of people. These makers are likely to seed shifts within large corporations as well as within communities. They will swap, build, and rebuild.

MAKERS IN THE FOOD WEB

Food has always been an interesting medium for expressing the maker instinct. Kitchens are designed for makers, with as much elegance and creativity as the cook (aka maker) would like. In the always-busy world of the future, the desire to prepare meals will be tempered by time. Although people want to be involved in making food for themselves and their families, they won't have hours to invest in cooking. Expect food retailers to respond with approaches to cooking that will allow people to participate in meal preparation, thus providing the psychological satisfaction of making their own food, without requiring the time to do so from scratch.

Founded by some of the team from *Wired* magazine, TCHO is a high-tech chocolate company in San Francisco, based on the idea of chocolate as a creative medium, with many different customization options. Customers are involved in creating their own chocolate without having to make it themselves. Consider how the maker instinct plays out at TCHO, based on how they describe themselves in these selections from their home page. Makers are often obsessed, very obsessed. Their customers can benefit from that obsession, as is clear from their principles:

TCHO is where technology meets chocolate; where Silicon
Valley start-up meets San Francisco food culture.

TCHO is an innovative method for you to discover the chocolate
you like best.

TCHO is scrappy and high-tech—recycling and refurbishing legacy chocolate equipment and mating it with the latest process control, information, and communications systems.

TCHO's social mission is the next step beyond Fair Trade— helping farmers by transferring knowledge of how to grow and ferment better beans so they can escape commodity production to become premium producers.

TCHO encourages our customers to help us develop our products, as we launch limited-run, "beta editions" available on our website.

TCHO creates new rituals for sharing chocolate.[3]

These TCHO principles reflect an emerging style of maker culture as it transforms into a sophisticated business. Notice the mix of maker instinct, leadership style, and professional expression. That's leadership with a maker attitude. Expect more efforts like this that allow the maker instinct to be played out in the experience of food.

MAKERS MEET LIGHTWEIGHT MANUFACTURING

Lightweight manufacturing will magnify the importance of makers of the future. Within the next ten years, desktop manufacturing will allow us to "print" other products similar to the way we print ink on paper now. For example, Chicago chef Homaro Cantu offers edible menus so that customers can taste dishes before ordering them. Using special ink-jet printing techniques, Cantu blends his own mixtures of fruits, meats, fish, and vegetables in a form that can be printed on paper and eaten.

"You can make an ink-jet printer do just about anything," says Cantu. He hopes that his idea may find its way into popular media. "Just imagine going through a magazine and looking at an ad for pizza. You wonder what it tastes like, so you rip a page out and eat it," says the chef who is working at perfecting the flavors and has applied for a patent on the technique.[4]

Homaro Cantu is an edgy hybrid maker with both information technology and cooking skills. Recently he brought edible menus to

FIGURE 6. Chef Homaro Cantu.[5] *Source:* Used with permission of Cantu Designs.

a workshop we conducted in London—they were tasty, but not an alternative to lunch. He also showed that with the right kind of printer one could receive sushi through the Internet. The next generation of makers will have a new tool set available, resulting in creations that at this point are hard to imagine. Desktop manufacturing will allow us to "print" food, 3-D objects, and other products we have yet to conceive. If you can print sushi and send it through the Internet, what will makers make next?

A Leader with Strong Maker Instinct

Founding publisher of *MAKE: Magazine* and creator of the Maker Faire, Dale Dougherty is a leader of makers with a very strong maker instinct himself. Through the Maker Faire he is giving everyone the chance to meet makers. He calls it a "world's fair by and for the people. It's not like institutions. It's not big companies bringing stuff. It's really individuals just saying, 'here's what *I* do!'"[6] Big companies can still play a role, however. For example, they often sponsor areas of the fair where makers show off what they have done with standard products. "Hacking" used to be a negative term, but the makers are recasting it. Manufacturers create products, but makers can add new life to them and even repurpose them for very different applications, if manufacturers are smart enough to listen and learn from this kind of grassroots innovation. Makers will reimagine products even if the manufacturers resist.

Inspired by the Maker Faire, TechShop is a shared space where makers can use advanced tools, learn from each other, and collaborate on new creations. Physical places like TechShop will combine with virtual resources such as online tool sharing to produce a powerful new mix of media for making.

Applying his maker instinct, his leadership instinct, and his instinct to teach, Dougherty has established the remarkable event now known as the Maker Faire. I expect more of these fairs and similar events as the maker instinct spreads do-it-ourselves wisdom throughout our business and social cultures.

Maker Instinct Summary

The maker instinct is part job and part hobby. Leaders with the maker instinct are able to approach their leadership with the commitment of a job and the energy of a hobby. The leaders of the future will kindle this maker energy in themselves and in others. They will make the future and connect with others in the making. Makers don't always know the answer, but they're working on it.

In times of great uncertainty, the maker instinct is what separates the leaders from the powerless. When leaders feel overwhelmed, they can become passive. When things are chaotic, makers will view the stir of uncertainty as unfrozen opportunities to start making something new. It is much better to make something than it is to sit back and wring your hands.

2

Clarity

Ability to see through messes and contradictions
to a future that others cannot yet see.
Leaders are very clear about what they are making,
but very flexible about how it gets made.

ON DECEMBER 17, 2007, I was at the end of a twenty-hour British Airways trip from San Francisco to Milan, via London. Just before
we landed, the flight attendant asked me to put away my laptop, so
I stood the computer on its side under the seat in front of me, right
up against its frame, which was not my usual habit. I was so tired
from the trip that I had lost the ability to think clearly.[1] When we
landed in Milan, I got caught up in the race for customs and left my
MacBook behind. I didn't realize I had lost it until later that night in

my hotel room when I was unpacking. What a shock! Still, I naively thought I would get it back quickly. I was at a very nice hotel and the concierge had a transcendent presence that assured me he could solve any problem elegantly. I slept pretty well, almost expecting that my laptop would be returned to me at the hotel the next morning. "Here you are, sir. Sorry for the inconvenience," the concierge would say as he delivered my laptop in a Four Seasons envelope.

No such luck. I kept calling the lost and found at Heathrow Airport and waiting for a response. Finally, after twenty-two days, I connected with a very nice person who said she would "take one last look" in what I imagined was a large pile of lost stuff. She returned saying there *was* a white Mac laptop in the pile. Did I know the serial number? I didn't, but I could describe the colorful stickers on the machine from a recent IFTF game experience. "You are *so* lucky," she said.

Routines lay the groundwork for clarity. Breaking my routine impaired my clarity of mind. In times of stress, it is very possible to lose clarity. Leaders can only make the future if they are clear about what they are making, so they will need standard practices as a base to build upon. Clarity will be particularly important since volatility, uncertainty, complexity, and ambiguity will naturally lead to confusion. When people are confused, they seek clarity.

Clarity is important for companies and for individuals. British Airways had an opportunity to deepen its relationship with me by helping me find my lost computer. Indeed, it should have been relatively easy for them, since they knew exactly where I was sitting and should have been able to connect the lost computer to me—based on where it was found. Unfortunately, the British Airways employees I interacted with did not have clarity about their customer relationship with me. A lost computer could have been an opportunity to build a positive customer relationship; I really needed their help. They should have a clear process to retrieve lost items and a commitment to returning them, although if they have such a process I certainly did not experience it. Instead, they made no apparent effort to get it back to me.[2] It seems that many airlines view lost luggage as a nuisance. A lost computer may be a nuisance to an airline, but it is critical for the customer who lost it.

Compare my experience with British Airways to the professional baseball park Safeco Field in Seattle, where the operations staff prides itself on returning lost items. They have a return rate of 80 percent for items left at the stadium, an area much bigger than an airplane. The Safeco Field operations staff has found that when a lost item is returned, the person is first very surprised and then becomes a dedicated fan for life. A company can view a lost item as a burden, or as an opportunity to grow a strong customer relationship. Clarity like this is key for companies and for leaders.

Although it has always been an enduring leadership trait, clarity will have new importance in the VUCA world. Global security will require new kinds of leadership. For example, the Bush administration's reasons for going into Iraq were very clear in advance, but their assessment regarding weapons of mass destruction was later proven to be inaccurate. Bush won a second term even after his decisions that led to the Iraq War were extensively debated and exposed as flawed. The electorate still decided that George Bush was clear and decisive, but John Kerry was not. Apparently the fact that Bush was clear was more important than the fact that he was wrong.

Both the good and bad sides of clarity will become increasingly apparent in the world of the future, even more apparent than they are today. Politicians will have a particularly difficult time being both clear and accurate—given the complexities that we will all be facing and the public demand for clarity. Some situations are *just not clear*, but it is hard for politicians to say that without recourse. When people are confused, they want clarity—even if it's wrong.

Clarity Defined

Clarity in leadership is the ability to

- See through messes and contradictions.
- See a future that others cannot yet see.
- Find a viable direction to proceed.
- See hope on the other side of trouble.

As volatility, uncertainty, complexity, and ambiguity increase, there will be many people wanting to be led out of the mess. Clarity will be a prerequisite for compelling leadership. As the world gets more confusing, it will become harder to see through to a better future. The best leaders are seers and sensors. The future will be loaded with contradictions, but leaders with clarity will need to see through those contradictions and have the ability to discern what to do and where to go, when neither is apparent. In order to grapple with complex questions, leaders will need to resist the temptation to oversimplify and give the easy answers that many people crave. One of the most difficult dilemmas for leaders will be providing clarity without inducing false hope. They will need to devise plans that are precise and simple. By combining wisdom from the past with a vision for the future they will need to navigate seemingly absurd situations and see the opportunities hidden within.

Clarity requires inner strength and discipline. Although they will no doubt experience hopelessness, leaders with clarity will still be determined to engage with the VUCA world and pull everything together in a way that is unmistakably practical.

Clarity requires great self-knowledge, so leaders will have to look within and sort out what is most important to them.

Clarity requires external engagement. Leaders must express themselves clearly in ways that inspire others to follow, and be able to make sharp statements about plans for the future with an enthusiasm that attracts others.

Clarity requires flexibility. The best leaders will be clear about their long-term intentions, but very flexible about how to get there. Clarity sets the parameters within which creativity can occur. As with jazz, the structure sets the limits within which improvisation is encouraged.

A stereotype is false clarity: an oversimplified label that puts a person or a group in a box. A stereotype presents the illusion of understanding, but is actually more likely to result in dangerous misconceptions and estrangement for both the person who is stereotyping and the one being stereotyped. Leaders should resist falling prey to stereotypes, but the future forces of the next decade will make that very difficult.

Leaders with clarity have authentic future intent. That is to say, they remain true to an inner purpose. One leader's clarity may make others uncomfortable or may even lead to polarization. Still, if all sides are clear, the disagreements will at least be authentic, and people want authenticity in their leaders.

Several years ago, my family went rafting on the Middle Fork of the Salmon River in Idaho. Our guide taught us to concentrate on the water that flowed through these world-class rapids, rather than on the rocks we wanted to avoid. I also learned that though it certainly does not offer control, the very act of paddling provides stability and some sense of direction. When you find yourself in extreme rapids, you must be clear about where you are going and keep paddling, no matter what.

Clarity in a business context is a precise statement of your strategy, sometimes called strategic intent. It lays out where you are going and how you intend to get there. Strategy thought leaders Gary Hamel and C.K. Prahalad talk about strategic intent as "an ambitious and compelling ... dream that energizes ... that provides the emotional and intellectual energy for the journey ... to the future."[3] They go on to describe how an effective strategic intent should not only indicate direction, but also relay a sense of discovery and even destiny. They are combining clarity with compelling engagement and aspiration to create effective leadership.

Willie Pietersen from Columbia Business School, a former CEO himself, emphasizes clarity when he talks about his notion of a Winning Proposition: what does a company do better than its competitors to give value to its customers as well as maintain successful financial performance? "If strategy is about winning, we need to be clear about the measures of success. In business, success means winning against the competition for value creation on two fronts: greater value for customers and greater profits for your company and its shareholders."[4] Pietersen says the Winning Proposition should be expressed in a concise phrase that brings clarity to life.

The Winning Proposition should be both clear and inspirational. The best ones demonstrate a very clear future intent, but they should also stretch everyone in the organization beyond the present toward a

FIGURE 7. Syngenta's Winning Proposition. *Source:* Used with permission of Syngenta.

desired future state. The Winning Proposition provides great flexibility for people to pursue the dream in varied ways. Consider the clarity in these statements from four very different big brand companies.

- Global branding agency Ogilvy & Mather: "The brand of choice for those who value brands."[5]
- Southwest Airlines: "On-time airline performance that rivals the cost of automobile travel, with a touch of fun."[6]
- Consumer products leader Procter & Gamble: ". . . improve the lives of the world's consumers, now and for generations to come." A related mantra is "The consumer is boss."[7]
- Agribusiness leader Syngenta: "Bringing plant potential to life."[8]

All of these companies are leaders in their industries. Each has a strong future orientation that is clearly articulated. A Winning Proposition does not guarantee success, but it positions companies very well for the uncertainties of the future. Even in a VUCA world, these companies know where they are going and how they are going to get there.

Clarity in Future Context

The next ten years look more complex to me than any future time period that I have studied in my career. There are so many variables at play, with such high stakes on a global scale. Sometimes, clarity will be both demanded and impossible to achieve. Absolute clarity will rarely be possible, particularly in this next decade, but it always will be possible to be more or less clear.

CLARITY INSIDE AND OUTSIDE DIASPORAS

Diasporas seem very clear to their own members, who share values and have similar worldviews, but to those attempting to look in, they can be opaque or even threatening. Because diasporas tend to be so inwardly focused, they are often difficult for others to understand. It is tempting for outsiders to oversimplify, which is the first step down the slippery slope toward stereotyping. Indeed, some diasporas define themselves as being profoundly different from the rest of the world, and some are exclusive and do not really want to be understood by outsiders. Some diasporas may only want clarity for themselves. Expect to see more diasporas with great power in the next ten years. Clarity in this complicated world of many different and sometimes-competing diasporas, however, will be elusive.

CLARITY IN WAR

Since 9/11, I have participated in a series of workshops with business executives, nonprofit administrators, and military leaders at the Army War College in Carlisle, Pennsylvania. We meet to compare approaches to strategy and leadership in our various fields of practice.

We meet to learn from each other. It is there that I learned about clarity in the world of warfare. They call it "commander's intent."

> The commander's intent describes the desired end state. It is a concise expression of the purpose of the operation and must be understood two echelons below the issuing commander . . . It is the single unifying focus for all subordinate elements . . . Its purpose is to focus subordinates on the desired end state.[9]

Commander's intent calls for a leader to be very clear about the end state desired but very flexible about how the soldiers in the field actually get to that clear end state.

Television viewers got an inside view of commander's intent when they watched the PBS ten-part series called *Carrier,* filmed aboard the USS *Nimitz*.[10] This documentary shows everyday life on a giant modern aircraft carrier. It shows how young people—many of whom came from troubled backgrounds and would have had difficulty landing jobs at most companies—have risen to the challenges presented on this very large and dangerous ship. Military personnel have principles and they have their commander's intent—which varies depending on the mission. Within the parameters of their commander's intent, individual crew members have freedom to improvise—and improvise they do, as *Carrier* reveals with great insight and humor. At the individual level, life on board leaves room for flexibility and personalization, while as a whole the crew moves ahead with clarity and purpose.

CLARITY IN FOOD SAFETY

My IFTF colleague Lyn Jeffery is a cultural anthropologist who has been doing research in China for many years. Fascinated with their culture and practices, she views people in China through the lens of the future. What do these practices say, Lyn asks, about possible threats and opportunities? In her studies of Chinese families a few years ago, she saw that more of them were buying vegetables wrapped in plastic, instead of buying them in the traditional open market setting with all the produce on display. As a good anthropologist is taught, Lyn tried to figure why these consumers had changed their behavior. Gradually, it became clear to her that these rural Chinese families were becoming concerned about the safety of their own food and no longer felt they could trust the food in the open market. They wondered if the efforts to control food quality were good enough and believed, perhaps incorrectly, that plastic-wrapped food was safer than produce purchased from open bins.

This ethnographic research was an early indicator of what has grown into a widespread concern about food safety—particularly the safety of food from China. More and more people now want to know where their food came from, how it was grown, and what happened to it before it got to them at the point of purchase. People want transparency with regard to their food, so they can have more confidence that what they are eating is at least safe. In the world of food, transparency is clarity.

In the simpler world of the past, the branding of food was all about look, feel, and taste. Does it look appetizing? Does it feel ripe? Does it taste good? As we grow up, we are all taught how to make those choices—although the guidance regarding what is good to eat varies dramatically from culture to culture. Now, the stakes seem higher. How do we make safe food choices from a food web that is increasingly suspect? Manufacturers need to assure consumers that their food is safe, or at least inform them of the risks so that they can make choices.

Leaders with Great Clarity

Leadership clarity is certainly not a completely new concept, even though the context of the future will make clarity much more difficult to achieve. Martin Luther King Jr. is a classic example of clarity, and his lessons are still very relevant today. Even in a book about leadership skills for the future, it is important to learn from leadership models of the past. Dr. King had a very effective way of making the future in the context of great clarity.

I went to divinity school in Chester, Pennsylvania, at Crozer Theological Seminary, where Dr. King went to seminary, and I was there when he was killed in 1968. To honor his legacy, the school designed a course that replicated the intellectual influences that Dr. King experienced in divinity school. Dr. Ken Smith, a Christian Ethics professor who had been one of Dr. King's mentors, taught the course, and I was fortunate to be one of the students.

Martin Luther King Jr. was very clear in his overall leadership direction, even though he was very flexible about his strategies and tactics. His roots compelled him to focus on human justice—wherever those issues arose. While he is known for his groundbreaking work on civil rights, he also took controversial stances on what he saw as related issues, such as the war in Vietnam and the budding ecology movement around the first Earth Day. Many said that Dr. King had lost focus and should concentrate on civil rights. He talked about that vision in his famous "I've been to the mountaintop" speech just before he was killed.[11] His vision was very clear for his followers, but his social change strategy evolved considerably as the civil rights movement took hold and other social issues joined the mix. His clarity focused on the Promised Land and human justice, while his tactics varied considerably in response to the challenges and opportunities of the time.

Nobel Prize-winner Muhammad Yunus is a current leader with clarity about social justice. Yunus developed the principles and practices of microfinance to help impoverished people help themselves. His approach is local, personal, and integrated with local communities. His model focuses on microcredit that allows someone with little or no resources to start a business, which creates an upward cycle of receiving income, investing more into the business, making a profit, and repaying the loan. He works with and grows social capital with small loans, primarily to women in local communities. Expressing his clarity about social justice, Yunus says, "One day our grandchildren will go to the museums to see what poverty was."[12]

Clarity in Summary

Leaders must have clarity to be successful in the VUCA world that we are already beginning to experience. They understand why people crave easy answers, but these leaders thrive in the space between hope and hopelessness—without overpromising. Clear-eyed leaders will experience hopelessness, but they won't accept it; they will see through it and be determined to make it otherwise. Leaders will immerse themselves in the VUCA world and—even if they become disoriented for a while—find a way to clarity.

3

Dilemma Flipping

Ability to turn dilemmas—

which, unlike problems, cannot be solved—

into advantages and opportunities.

———

The test of a first-rate intelligence is to hold two opposing ideas
in mind at the same time and still retain the ability to function.
One should . . . be able to see that things are hopeless yet
be determined to make them otherwise.

F. SCOTT FITZGERALD

———

HOLDING "TWO OPPOSING IDEAS" in mind will be even more important in the future than it was when Fitzgerald observed this in 1936. In fact, there will sometimes be more than two opposing ideas—all of which have some validity. Leaders will need to learn to like this space and make decisions, even when they cannot succeed by problem solving.

More volatility, uncertainty, complexity, and ambiguity means it will be harder to see through the mess. The dilemmas of the future will be more grating, more gnawing, and more likely to induce feelings of hopelessness. Leaders must be able to flip dilemmas over and find the hidden opportunities. They must avoid oversimplifying or pretending that dilemmas are problems that can be solved. Dilemma flipping is the recurrent skill that leaders (many of whom were trained as problem solvers) will need in order to win in a world dominated by problems that nobody can solve.

Many people will find it hopeless. Certainly, we all have those moments—and looking ahead ten years may spark more of them—but the lesson for future leaders: nurture the ability to engage with hopelessness, learn how to wade through it to the other side, and flip it in a more positive direction. Dilemma flippers turn hopelessness into hope.

My definition of a dilemma is a problem that cannot be solved and will not go away. The traditional definition of a dilemma was the choice between two equally bad options (often referred to as a "Hobson's Choice"). The challenge for leaders is to flip the dilemma into an opportunity. At Walt Disney World in Orlando, for example, standing in lines has always been a dilemma. Nobody likes to stand in line, and there is strong evidence that the guests are less patient than ever. Still, Disney doesn't want long downtimes when there is nobody ready to ride, so they make the waiting experience as pleasant as possible. They have made a number of attempts to flip the waiting dilemma, including video entertainment and indicators about how long the wait will be from a particular point. Another interesting innovation is Pal Mickey, a stuffed Mickey Mouse doll that entertains the kids and has a sensor in its nose that can pick up signals and tell the guest where lines are shorter. Theme parks will never solve the queuing dilemma, but they can make it a lot better.

Leaders in the corporate context can surely relate to the F. Scott Fizgerald quote about holding opposing ideas in tension. One such dilemma we see in business is balancing global scale and local customization. On the one hand, products and services need to be scalable in order to be on a growth path in terms of efficiency and return on investment. On the other hand, consumers in the next decade will increasingly desire products and services that feel local, even personalzed.

Leaders who exhibit dilemma flipping will find an opportunity in this tension, to explore new models of markets. Perhaps they will tap the market power of disporas, or engage with the Maker movement to offer products and services that are designed to be redesigned. Either way, these seemingly competing forces of global scale and local customization are not going away, and may even harbor great opportunity.

Another example of a dilemma: the balance of work and private life is impossible to achieve, at least in my experience. This is not a problem that can be solved. Rather, the intersection of the two is a territory that can only be navigated with assistance and intelligent choices. My wife is a lawyer who is always subject to the schedule of judges, and she rarely has control over her own calendar. My schedule has more flexibility, but I often have events scheduled months in advance and I don't have much slack in my calendar. Whenever we'd plan a vacation, one of us would come up with a fully legitimate reason why the trip was not feasible. It took a while for us to realize that this was not a problem, but a dilemma, which we flipped by finding an available place close to home that we both liked and was accessible on a last-minute basis. We traded off the possibility of more distant vacation sites, but we could take off spontaneously when time windows did appear. We have not solved this work/life challenge; we're just navigating it as best we can. And, occasionally, we get a last-minute special retreat we hadn't counted on—which makes it so much more delightful.

Another family dilemma that we had as our two kids were growing up was that there was no activity that we all liked to do, or even that both of our kids liked to do simultaneously. As they got older, this situation got worse, and we never seemed in sync for a family vacation. Our resolution—not a solution—was to take separate vacations where one parent would go with one kid. It turned out it was much easier to find something that one parent and one kid wanted to do than it was to find something that all four of us wanted to do and could schedule. We flipped the dilemma of finding something for all four of us to coming up with two activities, so that everyone was happier.

Leaders of the future will need to thrive in the world of modern dilemmas. Often, there will be more than two choices and they may not be equally bad. The good news is that dilemmas can present new opportunities to create win/win strategies, beyond the "I win/you lose" models common to the world of problem solving.

The dilemmas of the future will have the following characteristics:

- Unsolvable
- Recurrent
- Complex and messy
- Threatening
- Confusing
- Puzzling
- Potentially positive.[1]

Dilemma Flipping Defined

Dilemma flipping is reframing an unsolvable challenge as an opportunity, or perhaps as both a threat *and* an opportunity. It is the ability to put together a viable strategy when faced with a challenge. But first one must distinguish between a problem (that can be solved) and a dilemma (that cannot). Dilemma flipping is not a classical American trait. Henry Kissinger, a former U.S. Secretary of State and still a leading global policy analyst, observed:

> You Americans, you're all engineers. You think that all the worlds' problems are puzzles that can be solved with money and material. You are wrong. All the world's great problems are not problems at all. They are dilemmas, and dilemmas cannot be solved. They can only be survived.[2]

American leaders do tend to be problem solvers. They consider all the options, reduce them to two as quickly as possible, pick the best solution, and run in that direction, expecting to be evaluated by how fast they run.

A "flip" turns the dilemma around, to move from hand wringing to opportunity analysis. Dilemmas, particularly in the eyes of a problem solver, often seem overwhelming, but are rich in potential, though the opportunities are masked.

Dilemma flipping is not completely new. Consider the truth in these old adages: Is the glass half empty or half full? When life gives you lemons, make lemonade. Indeed, leadership has always been related to the ability to see something good where others see only limitations. In the future it will be much harder to find the silver linings—but they will be there. For example, employees in network-style organizations want to feel involved. Leaders must create a climate that delivers a feeling of involvement while also exerting strong leadership when that is needed. The demand for involvement will always be there, but the opportunities for leadership will be difficult to see and even more difficult to grasp.

Roger Martin calls this leadership ability the "opposable mind," an ability to engage constructively in the tension between opposing ideas and not be forced into premature choice or resolution. New ideas often emerge from conflict, but do not need to be resolutions. Martin's work on what he calls "integrative management" is inspirational for many leaders and highlights how the best of today's leaders strategize.[3]

But many people do not have "opposable minds" and cannot live with great levels of uncertainty. They need answers, even if there are none. The protective bubble of self-righteousness can insulate one from the outside world. From inside the bubble, the world may look wrong—but you feel right.

Dilemmas in the Future

If you look at the Ten-Year Forecast inside the book jacket, you will see dilemmas everywhere. Consider these:

DIASPORA DILEMMAS

Diasporas are complex, living, social networks that require nurturing and deep understanding as dynamic, organic, and extremely important phenomena. Diasporas are complex. Bonded by common values, diasporas help their members make sense out of the world around them and often guide members in very explicit ways.

Most leaders belong to at least one diaspora themselves; some leaders belong to many. Leaders need the ability to work across diasporas, however. We all need to move beyond the comfort of our own clan.

Dealing with a diaspora is tricky if you do not belong to it, or especially if you are a member of a competing one. Some were formed in response to a dominant group. They often have sharp distinctions between insiders and outsiders and sometimes distrust the latter. Some people are part of many different diasporas, which mix and overlap.

Diasporas not only raise dilemmas, they are dilemmas. They are too complicated to understand completely. You cannot think of them as static market segments; they are dynamic. You may be able to gain insight about one, but you will not be able to control it. Diasporas cannot be "solved" and they will not go away. In fact, they will grow in reach and power as they become more amplified by electronic media.

For example, corporate diasporas pose both a threat and an opportunity. Even as recently as ten years ago, most of our client companies did not stay in touch with their alumni. Their goal was to keep employees for as long as possible, but when they left, it was as if they had died. Losing an employee is a major cost for companies, since it is expensive to replace them. This negative, however, can be flipped into a positive. A former employee can become a new client.

Companies like McKinsey saw this opportunity early. They realized that when consultants left the firm there was a good chance that they would become clients of McKinsey. The more star consultants that McKinsey creates, the more those star consultants will seed other companies. Losing an employee to gain a client is often a great trade-off to make.

Now, a wide range of companies has active former employee networks, such as the Apple Alumni Association and the IBM Alumni Network. SelectMinds, for example, is a corporate social network company that supports large corporations who want to stay connected to former employees and others who are part of a corporate diaspora.[4] Of course, such organizations are a mixed blessing for many companies. They require constant nurturing and they can generate both positive and negative buzz. Still, sustaining the corporate diaspora is, in the long run, something that most companies should choose to do.

DILEMMAS OF WAR

Modern warfare is packed with dilemmas. That is why the Army War College is now calling itself informally "VUCA University." Warfare is always ugly, so an ugly acronym for volatility, uncertainty, complexity, and ambiguity is appropriate.

Traditional warfare was more comfortable for problem solvers. When one large state goes to war with another large state, there are clear rules of engagement. In a conflict where terror is a primary tactic and the enemy could be anyone, anytime, anyplace, there are no rules that are generally accepted. In fact, the various participants have different rules for engagement and different standards regarding what is appropriate and what is humane. To engage in such warfare is to engage with dilemmas. Hopelessness abounds. Creative courses of action appear, but they are often hidden in grief.

Over the next decade, network-based armies will seek to disrupt social, economic, and political systems through meme warfare. Memes are trigger thoughts that can spread rapidly. Rigid responses to this kind of threat can cripple the systems they are intending to protect. Resilient strategies that include great flexibility and ability to absorb disruption will work best. Economic markets, for example, are dependent on trust. Meme warfare would seek to undermine trust and spread a sense of worry and concern. It is hard to imagine how this could be flipped into an opportunity, but it is easy to imagine how it could disrupt markets.

An important part of resilience will be leaders who can engage with dilemmas and try to flip them into opportunities. For example, many local people in Iraq viewed American soldiers with skepticism, but there was always the possibility that skepticism could be turned around and built into trust—at least on a person-to-person basis.

A BOOMER-FUELED DILEMMA

As some humans struggle even to survive, other humans over the next decade will strive to become more than human, healthier than normal. In this context of crisis and reinvention, new dilemmas will arise for individuals and institutions.

The technologies of health are blossoming in new ways, just as the Baby Boomers are reaching what used to be called "retirement age." Most Boomers, however, don't want to retire even if they could afford it—and most of them cannot. A subset of this group is the richest cohort of retirees in history, which is doubly interesting since most of them won't actually retire. Instead, the Boomers will reshape the later years in life and reinvent retirement, just as they have had great influence on so many other social institutions as they have aged.

I expect a Boomer term to replace the word "retirement" within the next decade. My favorite candidate at this point is "refirement," but "redirection" and "regeneration" also capture some of the new concepts of aging. Many of the Boomers seem to view death as an option they are not planning to take. This mindset will create a rich market for death-avoidance techniques and technologies—at any price. A series of dilemmas will arise out of this vibrant yet futile quest:

FIGURE 8. A Boomers Forecast. *Source:* IFTF, *Boomers: The Next 20 Years,* 2007. SR# 1053.

- How can the best health care be delivered when there are limited resources to do it? Do just the rich get to live longer and in more comfortable ways?

- How will performance-enhancing drugs be handled in the workplace, where drugs of some kinds are not allowed? In sports, performance-enhancing drugs are typically outlawed, but what about in offices? In the next decade, new drugs could allow longer work hours on less sleep, for example. Do leaders allow such drugs? Might some leaders require them?

- How do leaders encourage healthy lifestyles without invading the privacy of workers? For example, if a rising star leader *looks* overweight (looking overweight does not necessarily mean someone is at an unhealthy weight that might affect performance), is that enough to discourage a promotion? Can a leader require healthy behavior, since physical health does contribute positively to leadership performance?

Problems Disguised as Dilemmas

If you are lucky, you will experience situations that look to you like dilemmas, yet when you flip them you will find a solution on the other side. Don't expect this kind of luck in the VUCA world of the future, but enjoy it when it happens.

For example, my mom called me recently to report that her ceiling fan had stopped working. In order to diagnose what was wrong, the fan company needed the serial number of the fan's motor. To find the serial number I would need to climb up to the ceiling and look on top of the fan. I climbed cautiously up a ladder to the ceiling fan, only to discover that the fan's motor was so close to the ceiling that when I tried to squeeze my head in the small space between the fan and the ceiling, the sticker with the serial number was too close to my face to read the numbers. Hmm . . . . I thought: how could I fit my head in that tiny space so I could read the number? Use a mirror? Try tilting the fan so I could read the serial number? This puzzle seemed like an everyday household dilemma to me and I was ready to stretch my creativity to get that number.

About that time, my mom asked quietly, "Could you remove the sticker?" My mom, in her own humble way, had flipped the dilemma I was working on by reframing it as a problem that could be solved.

Another more historic example of a problem disguised as a dilemma comes from World War II. General George Patton, during the German invasion of France, came upon his staff as they were plotting strategy. Patton's staff leaders were depressed by the hopelessness of the current troop placements they were analyzing, which showed that the Allied Forces were completely encircled by German troops. Patton looked at the same hopeless troop configurations and said something like: "They've got us surrounded again, poor bastards."[5] Patton saw that by surrounding the Allied Forces, the Germans had thinned their resources so that U.S. troops could break through the German circle and gain an advantage. He saw where the enemy was strong, but he also saw where his own leaders were weak: their point of view was limited. Where Patton's staff interpreted the situation as hopeless, Patton saw it as an opportunity for a new kind of attack. He flipped the dilemma they were facing by seeing the same data in a very different way. Patton didn't win the war right there (that is, he didn't solve the German Problem), but he certainly improved that battle situation. Being surrounded is only hopeless if you stay where you are. That logic is likely to apply in the future, just as it did in the past.

Dilemma flipping is an everyday skill. The world of today can be a practice ground for the future. Unfortunately, many dilemmas in the future will not be able to be flipped into solvable problems—such as reading the serial number on the fan—but they usually can be flipped in a way that makes the situation better.

In the future world there will still be problems and it will be important to solve those that can be solved. Typically, however, top leaders will assign people to solve the problems, and they will tackle the dilemmas themselves. Of course inside much larger dilemmas there will be many little problems.

Problem solving works when the parameters of a situation are clear and there is a problem that can be solved. Most future leaders will never experience a mature industry that is predictable and slow moving.

A Dilemma-Flipping Leader

Shortly after A.G. Lafley became the CEO of Procter & Gamble (P&G) in 2000, he visited the Institute for the Future and expressed a concern: research and development (R&D) was very important to P&G, but it was also quite expensive and not productive enough. While P&G is known for its marketing and advertising, it also has a massive commitment to science. P&G is known for hiring great scientists who create the base innovations for its products.

When I began working with P&G in 1977, my first assignment was to help them assess how the ARPAnet (the predecessor to the Internet) could be used to improve the R&D productivity of the "invisible college" of P&G scientists worldwide. "Invisible college," a term commonly used at the time in the literature of sociology of science, refers to the notion of scientists linked across physical distance. P&G had researchers around the world, but their emphasis was on the invisible college of scientists *within* P&G. Now P&G reaches far beyond their internal scientists to seek out and improve product ideas. In those days, when a scientist joined P&G or most other large science-based companies, they more or less withdrew from the open scientific communities in the universities in which they were trained. Now P&G scientists participate much more actively in the external world of science.

In 1977, IFTF was doing pilot tests of group communications media in use by defense contractors on the ARPAnet, who were the only people allowed to use the network in those early pre-Internet days. Within P&G's community of scientists, we were able to prototype a similar medium that eventually grew into a very large network. In fact, P&G is the only organization I know that created a group communications environment (akin to what we would call a wiki today) in the late 1970s before it adopted email.

P&G had a big dilemma in the year 2000: it had a very large R&D infrastructure that was a major overhead cost. Ideas were being generated, but not with the frequency or impact that Lafley wanted. Of course, P&G wanted to own or at least benefit from the new ideas it developed, but it also wanted to benefit from outside ideas. A.G. Lafley looked around at the decaying structure of research laboratories across industries around the world and asked if there was a better way. He valued—and he still values—the importance of science in P&G businesses. His dilemma was how to keep R&D a priority while moving into a new model of how it was conducted.

He explored many different models, including those common in Silicon Valley. Gradually, as his ideas about the future of R&D took shape and as Gil Cloyd became his Chief Technology Officer, the "Connect + Develop" strategy emerged. Connect + Develop is essentially an open model for innovation in science and product development. Instead of viewing science as something that happens inside P&G and moves to the outside only in the form of finished products, P&G reframed the R&D dilemma as an open network challenge. Of course there would be new issues of intellectual property and ownership in this new environment, but there would also be a much wider range of resources from which P&G could draw.

I was surprised in 2006 when P&G published its strategy about

Connect + Develop.[6] I knew about the P&G strategy, but assumed that I knew it under nondisclosure. At the time that I started working with P&G, it was very secretive and its R&D productivity was concentrated within the company. Now, with Connect + Develop, Lafley has reframed the community of scientists to include those outside P&G. By leveraging the external world of science, companies can innovate faster with less internal investment. This model of R&D still requires investment, but it is able to cast a much wider net for opportunities and resources.

A. G. Lafley did not "solve" the problems of cost, productivity, and intellectual property issues of R&D, but he did reimagine what was possible. His clear and public challenge to P&G was to derive half of the company's new product ideas from the outside world. This goal has now been achieved and publicly celebrated.[7] This new approach to R&D has increased its productivity for P&G. Lafley flipped the traditional notion of R&D into a much more open source and flexible network model.

I wish there were a hundred examples of leaders like A. G. Lafley, but I have not been able to find them. The ability to thrive in the space between judging too soon and deciding too late is rare. Dilemma flippers must love the process of puzzling—not *just* the outcome. You cannot, however, enjoy the process so much that you don't make decisions and act. Even in a world of dilemmas, leaders must decide.

Dilemma Flipping Summary

Dilemma flipping begins with a mind reset. As Winston Churchill once said, "The empires of the future are the empires of the mind."[8] Indeed, dilemma flipping is an ability that lives in an empire of a leader's mind—your own mind.

Dealing with dilemmas requires an ability to sense, frame, and reframe the situation. Reframing is stepping back, checking assumptions, and considering other ways of looking at a situation to see what's really going on. Often, dilemma flipping will require you to "remake" a situation. Remaking is reimagining and making again.

Making the future starts with making sense. Of course, with some dilemmas, there is little sense to be made. The best leaders stay alert and are sensitive to their environments, but they keep an open mind about what they are sensing and what it could mean. Often, leaders will not understand exactly what is going on in the present, but they will have to decide on a direction anyway.

At IFTF, we have found that foresight is a particularly good way to help see through dilemmas—even if you don't agree with the forecast. The big-picture view of a forecast frames the overall direction and what is possible. Once you discern what's going on and what *could* happen if you intervene with the right action at the right time, you are more likely to see through the dilemma. Often, the path is not clear until you stop thinking and start doing. Getting there early gives you time to sort things out, to reflect, and to plan your strategy.

To improve your own dilemma flipping abilities, try these three steps.

- First, identify your dilemma. If you are not sure if you are dealing with a problem or a dilemma, it is better to assume it is a dilemma. If it turns out to be a problem you can solve, just solve it. If, on the other hand, you mistake a dilemma for a problem, you may be in deep trouble by the time you realize your mistake. If others expect you to come up with a solution and you don't, it is hard to recast the situation as one that you cannot solve after all. Often the lack of distinguishing problems from dilemmas gets classified by the popular media as "flip-flopping."[9] Mistaking a dilemma for a problem can lead to this perception—perhaps with good reason.

- Second, immerse yourself in the dilemma (as I will discuss in more detail in chapter 4). This allows you to listen to and learn about what is going on within the frame of the dilemma—without jumping to a conclusion. Immersion also allows you to look for patterns and ways of making some sense out of what is going on. This is the space that leaders in the future must learn to love, but which problem solvers will have an urge to pass through as quickly as possible.

- Finally, flip the dilemma in a more positive direction. Dilemmas don't go away, but a leader can learn to reframe them and then reimagine the apparent contradictions in a way that leads to new opportunities that others don't yet see.

Leaders of the future must revel in the space between judging too soon and deciding too late, leaning toward action.[10] Judging too soon is the classic mistake of the problem solver, who has an urgent inner drive to solve. It is also a common error of people who *know* the answer before they consider the question. Many people with fundamentalist leanings, for example, are very comfortable judging others. Fundamentalism can be comforting psychologically, but it can be dysfunctional socially—especially if a group moves over the threshold of self-righteousness from being confident they are right to knowing everyone else is wrong.[11] Atheists can be just as sure as fundamentalists that they know the truth. Knowing too soon is also characteristic of the atheist. Careful reflection is critical in the decision-making process, so you don't judge prematurely and risk judging incorrectly.

Dilemmas require that you live with the uncertainty of the dilemma for a while before you decide what to do. Deciding too late is the classic mistake of those who love to study but have trouble getting around to deciding what to do with their research results. Deciding too late is also a challenge for the passively agnostic person who gets stuck in questioning mode. Leaders need to lean toward action, since leaders—unlike many academics or agnostics—are decision makers and must decide, even in face of dilemmas. Leaders cannot just lean back and ponder the resolvability of a dilemma indefinitely. They can ponder for a while, but they cannot *just* ponder. They still have to decide.

Dilemma flipping happens in the space between judging too soon and deciding too late. Leaders in the future must learn to love this space, without staying there too long. Reflection without judgment is necessary to engage with a dilemma, but the flip is a decision to act based on your reflection.

4

Immersive
Learning Ability

Ability to immerse yourself in unfamiliar environments,

to learn from them in a first-person way.

IF YOU ARE TRYING to help people relieve their knee pain, the best way to learn about that pain is to experience it yourself. Dr. Scott Dye did just that. He is an associate clinical professor of orthopedic surgery at UCSF and runs the San Francisco Knee Clinic. In 1997, Dr. Dye had both of his own healthy knees "inspected" without anesthetic (that is, cut open and probed for pain sensitivity by an orthopedic colleague) so that he could answer the following question personally and very specifically: what are the sources of pain in the knee? Dr. Dye describes his pain-seeking immersive experience with charming academic understatement in a medical journal article:

> Penetration of the unanesthetized anterior synovium and fat pad region during the initial examination of the right knee produced severe pain that elicited involuntary verbal exclamations from the subject [Dr. Dye himself] and nearly resulted in the cessation of the study. Further documentation of this sensory finding in the left knee was thought to be unnecessary.[1]

Based on his own immersion experience, Dr. Dye came up with a familiar analogy to share what he had felt with his patients. He likened the pain to what you feel when you bite your cheek. The swelling after the bite makes it very difficult to avoid reinjuring the cheek and it hurts terribly when you bite down on the sore.

To learn how to help people with knee pain, Dr. Dye immersed himself in that pain and documented his experience—to the point of "involuntary verbal exclamation"—and he figured out a way to communicate that experience to his patients. As a result, he redesigned treatment for knee pain and is now a leader in the field of knee pain relief.

Thankfully, there are ways to do immersive learning other than getting your knees cut open without anesthetic. Variants of simulation and gaming are the low-risk pedagogy of choice, a practical way for leaders to experience the future before it happens. Growing up playing video games could be very helpful for prospective leaders since serious gamers have the chance to immerse themselves in dilemmas and learn advanced social networking skills. Gaming and simulation are low-risk–high-return learning mediums, if used in a constructive fashion. They provide mind expansion and leadership skill development, even as they allow for exposure to overt violence and sexuality.

Grand Theft Auto has been widely criticized for its over-the-top violence and random sexuality. Serious players, however, can play this game with less violence, though it is impossible to play it without any at all. The medium is extremely rich, but the games themselves provide the content and context. *Grand Theft Auto* also has amazing visual virtual reality rendering of the cityscapes and provides so many options that there are infinite ways to play. The stories embedded in the game may not be that compelling, but the patterns of play can be remarkably complex and dilemma ridden. Gaming allows players to experience alternative worlds in a low-risk way. I believe—although I'm sure that many parents would be skeptical—that serious gamers will have an edge when they apply for leadership positions in the future. The key is whether or not they have learned the skills of dilemma engagement and social networking that many online games teach implicitly. For example, academic gaming researchers Constance Steinkuehler and Sean Duncan studied *World of Warcraft* players and found that they were developing very sophisticated mathematical models as part of their strategies for play and were also learning the basics of scientific thinking—in spite of what they and their parents thought they were doing. At least *some* serious gamers are "practicing scientific habits of mind in virtual worlds."[2] There is hope for worried parents of serious gamers.

Immersive learning can also happen in the world of new media and the practices that have grown up around them, such as social networking, social bookmarking, instant messaging, and tagging. Immersive online environments can be a safe place to practice leadership skills. Leaders don't have to adopt every model they come across, but it is important that they explore and understand what they can and cannot do. At least, leaders should encourage others to explore online social worlds so they have some organizational intelligence. Reacting with fear or disdain to new technologies and media (and the ecosystem of social and cultural practices that surround them) is precisely what a leader should not do. Engagement with gaming environments and encouraging (not just accepting) similar immersion among those being led will be an important dimension of leadership. Social networks are necessary to succeed.

The game playing style is also a critical element in what gets learned. Parents often ask me what to do about their children's desire to play video games. I recommend that they learn to play them with their children. Video games provide great opportunities for reverse mentoring where the kids teach the parents. The parents can also teach and demonstrate their values in their styles of play. Think of video games as dangerous but interesting urban neighborhoods. You can either forbid your children from going there or go there with them to help them develop their own safe practices. I recommend the latter. Learn from your kids, as you hope they will learn from you.

Immersive learning ability is more than the willingness to use online immersions, simulation, and gaming. It can be simply going into a world that is different for you. Recently, for example, I was doing a keynote talk in Orlando, Florida, for an industrial cleaning products company. I came in the evening before and was invited to go out with the top leadership team. Usually this sort of meeting would be at some upscale restaurant or resort retreat. This time we gathered in front of our hotel and boarded vans to a local $40 per night motel where this company's industrial cleaning products were being used.

When we arrived, we huddled in the parking lot with the lead sales person for that account and were herded into the laundry room to see how their cleaning products were used with soiled sheets and towels. Then we were each given a cleaning cart and taught how to clean authentically dirty motel rooms that had been "rented" for the occasion by the company who manufactures the cleaning products. I was taught, along with the top executives and the CEO of the company, how to use each of the products to clean very dirty rooms. Our assignment during this immersion was to finish one room every twenty minutes—the time budgeted per room for the people who do it every day. It is very difficult to clean a dirty motel room in twenty minutes, I learned. The motel was happy to rent the rooms for this purpose, but they did send people back to re-clean the rooms after we were done. Having done some questionable cleaning in the rooms where I was assigned, I think that was a wise choice. Cleaning motel rooms is very hard work!

I stay in hotel rooms often, but I had never cleaned one. This simple immersion experience changed the way I look at and experience hotel rooms. I learned how hard it is to follow the correct cleaning instructions, especially those regarding sanitation and disinfecting.

I learned how hard it is to do a good job cleaning a hotel room in twenty minutes. I learned how dirty some people leave their hotel rooms. I've always left tips in my hotel rooms for cleaning people, but having experienced just a taste of their everyday lives, I now leave a much larger tip.

My learning was less important for the company, however, than was the learning of the top executives who cleaned rooms alongside me. Will they make better business decisions because of this experience? I think so. Executives need to be able to put themselves in the shoes of the people using their products. These executives don't usually stay in $40 per night motels, and they certainly don't clean them.

This outing provided valuable information about the product. For example, the directions for use of the cleaning products were just not clear. The cleaning staff at that motel was made up mostly of people whose first language was not English. The directions for the cleaning products need to be in the language with which they were most comfortable—or better yet, in a very clear visual format that works across languages. Immersion experiences can change your life in tangible ways. It is always a good idea to learn from the people who use your products.

Immersive Learning Ability Defined

Immersion is close-up engagement in a world that is different from your own, whether it is a virtual world or just a world with which you are not familiar. Immersive learning ability sounds kind of fuzzy for a future leadership skill, but—depending on where you immerse yourself—experiences like these are likely to be both vivid and deeply memorable.

I use the term immersive broadly to include a wide range of learning environments, such as the following:

SIMULATIONS OF REALITY

Some aspects of the real world can be modeled so that they can be experienced in a low-risk way. Direct simulation of the real world is very difficult to achieve in most situations, but is sometimes possible; and the attempt to mimic is worthwhile even if the result only approximates reality. Simple realities can be duplicated, but the more complex the reality, the harder it is to reproduce. Some simulations are designed to be more difficult than reality, so that it will be easier for participants in the real world than it was in the game. In the world of leadership, full-scale simulations of reality are rare because the real-life choices leaders make are so difficult to replicate.

ALTERNATE-REALITY GAMES

Individuals, small groups, or massive numbers of players can engage in hypothetical worlds, either in digital environments or in physical space. An alternate-reality game is not necessarily a simulation of anything real, but it is a compelling immersive environment with challenges—again, a low-risk world where people can learn in a first-person way. In these games, people "play" themselves in an unusual and often playful setting. Jane McGonigal, one of the world's leading game designers who is now at IFTF, calls this "real-play," not role-play—since you play yourself.[3] Alternate-reality games combine elements of games with the real world to create a different setting.

3-D IMMERSIVE ENVIRONMENTS

People can become other people in an online setting. There is no story and no game in these worlds other than what the players themselves create. For example, young people who have forms of autism use 3-D immersive environments like *Second Life* to practice social skills. Expect to see many more 3-D immersive environments in the future.

ROLE-PLAY SIMULATION GAMES

Learners play roles in interactive simulations that draw from real-world experiences, giving them a taste of new situations and a chance to practice possible responses. Role-plays can be either more or less realistic and can allow leaders to learn for themselves without being themselves.

SCENARIOS

A scenario is a story brought to life in order to animate a forecast and engage with the users. For example, digital stories are short visual scenarios that can bring aspects of a forecast to life during a presentation. A text scenario may be more like a story from the future, while a physical one could be more like an artifact.

MENTORING, REVERSE MENTORING, OR SHADOWING

Learners can immerse themselves for a period of time in the life of another person from whom they want to learn. For example, some corporations have used reverse mentoring to help male managers get a taste of what female managers experience, to help white managers understand what managers of color experience, or to help older managers know what it's like for someone recently hired. In Europe, this practice is called a *secondment*, and it is often done in the early stages of someone's career.

AD HOC IMMERSIVE EXPERIENCES

The goal of such an experience is to help someone see the world from another point of view, as I did when I cleaned motel rooms. Think anthropology light, since the goal is similar to what anthropologists would call ethnography: a researcher becomes immersed in a culture to qualitatively understand it. Whereas an anthropologist goes deep for an extended time, an ad hoc immersive experience is just a quick taste—but it is a firsthand and potentially useful taste nonetheless. Ad hoc immersion experiences are similar to simulations, but they are much less ambitious since no imaginary world is created. Special body suits have been designed with weights and awkward padding, for example, to give young people a sense of what it feels like to be inside an older body. Other special suits have been designed to give men some sense of what is like to have a menstrual cycle or to begin to understand what it is like to be pregnant in the later stages.

THEATRICAL IMPROVISATION

Actors bring a future possibility to life in a vivid way while learners watch. These experiences can be more or less elaborate and vary on the degree of learner involvement. When the actors can engage with the learners, the learning opportunities are most profound. On several occasions, I have used actors in prototype homes or stores of the future to show how consumers might use them. For example, in a CEO Forum sponsored by P&G at Cambridge Business School in 2000, we used actors to show how consumers might behave. In this case, we felt it would be difficult to get the CEOs to role play, but using actors was a more realistic demonstration than giving a presentation.

CASE STUDIES

A real-world situation is described in an engaging way so that learners can become involved with the case. Case studies have a long history and much current practice in business schools (with many different approaches), so most people have become comfortable with it as a learning method. Case studies are engaging for the students who write them, but less so for the readers. They can be presented, however, in very engaging ways by skilled professors. You can read case studies and they are better than abstract anecdotes, but you can't experience them unless you have some kind of immersion experience as well.[4]

Dilemmas in the Future

Immersion is the learning medium of choice for the world of the future. You must experience something in order to learn it well, to learn it viscerally. It is much easier to make a future if you've had at least a taste of it. Finding your own clarity about options is much easier if you dive into possible future worlds.

IMMERSION DURING CRISIS SITUATIONS

Climate disruption diasporas, or large numbers of people who are forced to move by a storm or other natural disruption, are likely to become more common in the future. The Hurricane Katrina diaspora, for example, resulted in first an exodus of people from New Orleans and then their multiple migrations across the United States. Katrina's many tragedies became shared life-changing experiences

FIGURE 9. Tide's Mobile Laundromat for Hurricane Katrina survivors.[5]
Source: "Loads of Hope" used with permission of Tide.

that created strong social bonds. The Katrina diaspora was abruptly
separated from New Orleans. Many wanted to return but could
not. Now, gradually, New Orleans is being rebuilt and the Katrina
diaspora is taking on new shapes and forms. The post-Katrina world
is now loaded with immersion experiences.

Relief workers went to New Orleans for years after the storm to
help rebuild. There was so much work and it was likely to go on for
such a long time that churches and government agencies set up temporary housing for them. For the volunteers, rebuilding New Orleans
is a life-changing experience, an immersion in a broken world that
is coming back together. It was a chance to make a difference in a
disaster that caused a feeling of helplessness for many.

In the aftermath of Katrina, Procter & Gamble sent in large trucks
with washers and dryers and gave people Tide detergent so they
could wash their clothes right on the truck, giving many survivors
their first opportunity to have clean clothes in a long time in very hot

and sticky weather. This was a startling concept: an immersion experience in a branded laundry detergent. In the context of the extreme needs after Katrina, laundry detergent—something ordinarily taken for granted—took on dramatic new value. P&G will be regarded positively for being very responsive to this disaster, but a secondary benefit to the company was a chance to introduce the brand experience to thousands of people who were then likely to buy Tide after the crisis was over. Brand loyalty toward Tide within the Katrina diaspora spread quickly, as ideas always do within diasporas.

FINANCIAL IMMERSIONS

Financial planning is not one of my strong skill sets. I've had two recent immersion experiences in my own finances that are helping me prepare for my next phase of life.

IFTF uses TIAA/CREF, the pension planning organization for many universities and nonprofits. As I approached sixty, TIAA/CREF assigned a planner to me. She works mostly with people my age or older from Stanford and SRI International, as well as other nonprofits. As part of this program, she basically immersed me in my own finances. She used a simulation to play out alternative scenarios for the coming years, based on my priorities and things that could happen outside of my control. She placed my family and me in our own future world— actually several possible future worlds—and helped us make choices. Because things keep changing, we update that plan every year.

In parallel, our family broker at A.G. Edwards invited me to St. Louis, where the company uses immersion experiences as a way of helping people approaching retirement to consider their options. They also create a hypothetical world to help you explore your options. Actually going to another city is part of the experience—to get you out of your home and away from your usual ways of thinking. Personal finances are important, but until this trip I just could not bring myself to spend much time thinking things through. This immersion experience got me out of my normal space and into a new one that provided information and prompted more informed action on my part.

IMMERSION IN CIVIC ISSUES

The probability of a major earthquake in California over the next ten years is very high. Earthquake preparedness, however, is something that is difficult to promote—unless there has been a major earthquake recently. American Red Cross Bay Area is using a fascinating approach that is essentially an immersion experience in the impacts of an earthquake. A vivid and greatly enlarged photograph of the San Francisco Ferry Building in flames and falling is positioned on one side of the back of a large flatbed truck which is parked right in front of the Ferry Building. For an instant, passersby see the image of the collapsing Ferry Building, and it looks real. The message from the Red Cross Bay Area is simple: "What do we have to do to get your attention? Be prepared." On the other side of the truck is a similar photograph of Market Street. This immersion experience is memorable, but takes no effort on the part of the participants other than walking by and looking, and it is compact enough that it can go right out in the midst of people.

Another interesting example of this kind of street theater immersion is the work of Justin "Projekt" Rowley in San Francisco, who uses tape on lampposts to designate the future sea level in the South of Market area after the effects of global warming have taken effect. Of course, the future sea level is debatable, but the tape is striking and it certainly gets conversations going among people walking down the street—which is the point of this kind of immersive street art. The result is a vivid immersion experience in this topic and this art, just by walking by and looking.

IMMERSION IN NEW COMMONS

Institute for the Future has had a long-term interest in immersion experiences as a way of evaluating and trying out alternative scenarios. Just before IFTF was founded in 1968, two of our founders, Olaf Helmer and Ted Gordon, designed a board game called *Futures,* which created a cross-impact matrix of future events and their interactions. In 1979, we made a game called *Spinoff,* which immersed people in a multimedia world where they had to choose among face-to-face,

FIGURE 10. Superstruct, a simulation game for forecasting the future. *Source:* IFTF, Superstruct, 2008. SR# 1176.

audio, video, and computer-based teleconferencing (what would now be called a wiki) to resolve a crisis simulation.[6]

Gaming has become a platform for forecasting. IFTF's resident game designer, Jane McGonigal, with Ten-Year Forecast leaders Kathi Vian and Jamais Cascio, created an immersion experience that contributed to the annual Ten-Year Forecast for 2009-2019. The first simulation of this kind was called Superstruct (for superstructure, within which planning and choices for action are made) and was played in the fall of 2008 over a two-month period. It allowed thousands of people to participate in the Ten-Year Forecasting process.[7]

A Ten-Year Forecast can include a commons on which a wide variety of organizations can build. As the future gets more complex, there will be new challenges to create commons for base forecasting and frameworks for choice making. Superstruct is a kind of commons, a platform for forecasting and exchanging information about forecasts. It is also a place to try out new ideas about the future. Within the game, participants can fast-forward ten years in their own lives to imagine a range of options. What external challenges will they face? What kind of person and what kind of leader do they want to become?

Superstruct was a real-play game, taking a step beyond role-play games by inviting participants to be themselves in a future world where they can grow their own skills and explore new social possibilities.

Games like Superstruct build on a tradition of socially constructive gaming that began to blossom with *SimCity,* the very successful Will Wright game that presents players with social dilemmas for which there are no clear solutions. Players are immersed in decisions that are like those faced by city planners and others who create shared public spaces. *SimCity* is one of the early pioneering efforts to simulate the real world in such a way that players can learn in a low-risk manner. Leadership in the future will require new strategies and tactics. You will still have to learn as you go, but gaming can help you do some learning *before* you go.

IMMERSION BEFORE AND AFTER WARFARE

Doug Campbell, chief war-gaming puppet master at the Army War College, likes to say, "Simulation builds calluses." Indeed, the essence of military pedagogy is simulation and other forms of immersion; and immersion is the essence of the learning transformation that the army and other military agencies have gone through since the Vietnam War. The big incentive to learn in immersive worlds is that you can practice without the risk of getting hurt physically. You can even experience being killed without having to die. Games are an excellent way to learn about war in a low-risk setting, to develop your own leadership style, and to grow those calluses before you get into battle.

Anne Lilly Cone, a consumer insights leader at Procter & Gamble, points out that, beyond calluses, immersion experiences build muscle. They give leaders a chance to experiment and learn in realistic but not real settings. War gaming is typically designed to make the simulation harder than the real world, so that when a soldier is actually in a battle, it is easier than expected—even though the stakes have become much higher. In the Iraq War soldiers are taught with immersion experiences through war games at the army's National Training Center in the Mojave Desert for two weeks, twenty-four hours a day, in the world's largest video gaming parlor (about the size of Rhode Island).

Simulation has obvious benefits in training people for war, but it also seems to be useful to help people recover from war. Simulation is being tested as part of what is sometimes called "immersion therapy" for Iraq veterans returning with post-traumatic stress disorder. The Virtual Iraq virtual reality game is modeled on an earlier game called Virtual Vietnam as well as a current video game called Full Spectrum Warrior. Virtual Iraq reimmerses veterans in the frightening world of war that they are trying to return from both physically and psychologically. Working with trained therapists in a safe environment, soldiers are able to relive those awful moments that they cannot get past when they return to life off the battlefield. For many of these returned soldiers, their minds have been *dis*ordered by ugly experiences and they must *re*order when they return. The idea is to revisit the negative experiences and learn how to isolate those cues from a psychological chain of negative reactions. Immersion experiences, coupled with therapy, can help traumatized soldiers to come to grips at their own pace in a low-risk virtual world. One of the therapists testing the new game summarizes the challenge: "Because numbness and avoidance are symptoms of PTSD, you're asking the person to do in treatment the very thing their mind is avoiding doing. That's quite a dilemma."[8]

A CEO'S IMMERSION EXPERIENCE WITH A SHOPPER

Immersion experiences are important for leaders so they can see the world as others see it. On a recent occasion, I went on an immersive shopping experience with the CEO of a larger consumer products company. A market research company paired us anonymously with a young single mom living on an annual income of $50,000 in the upscale peninsula region of the Bay Area. The CEO was surprised to see that the mom did not choose any of his company's products, but he got a firsthand sense as to *why* when he went around the store with the mom and her three restless kids. A $50,000 income still seems like a lot of money to many people, but not for a single mom in San Mateo.

Things are changing so fast that leaders need to immerse themselves in the currents frequently to grasp the points of view of people who are most important to them.

IMMERSION IN AMPLIFIED ORGANIZATIONS

Alegent Health in Omaha, Nebraska, has created a "Decision Accelerator" space in one of its buildings. From the outside, it looks like a typical suburban office building. Inside, however, it is very different. Alegent wanted to get people out of their normal constraints, amplify their everyday ways of thinking, break patterns of thought. Everything in the Decision Accelerator is flexible. The furniture is movable so that it can be reconfigured easily, and most things are on wheels. Also in the space are facilitators and artists who can help visualize the ideas. The vision is both to speed up decisions and reframe those decisions in ways that might be more productive for Alegent and for its community.

The Decision Accelerator is an immersion in a different kind of decision making. By going there, a group is saying that it is open to ideas that are out of the ordinary, and perhaps better. The Accelerator stretches thinking and presses for something better—but leaves it up to the groups to make those changes. It immerses groups in a different space to provoke alternate ways of thinking and speed up the overall process in a way that leads to improved results.

A Leader with Strong Immersive Learning Ability

Doug Campbell is the lead gamer at the Army War College, a place where games of war—and peace—happen all the time. A former cavalryman, Campbell walks with a limp and is missing a finger from an accident. He is a crusty, down-to-earth, friendly genius who lives gaming. I've been in a number of simulations with him, and he is incredibly engaged and animated. I was at the Army War College when he conducted a two-week global crisis simulation. During the entire time, Professor Campbell had a headset on to follow the play of the game, while also navigating his real-life duties, including talking to me periodically. I was not his priority during the game, nor should

I have been, but he was still able to multi-process in multiple realities with remarkable grace.

Doug Campbell's war gaming includes a range of different experiences, such as NATO war-gaming in Europe. At the Army War College, he makes the immersion as much like the real world as possible while also stretching the scenario ten years ahead in the world of warfare. He has an amazing ability to do that, like a good trainer stretches an athlete before a game. Sometimes he gives demonstration immersion experiences to business executives, nonprofit leaders, and military commanders. At one of these sessions, he allowed us to play an abbreviated version of the global crisis simulation. It was an experience that provided us all with an immersion in the awkward sticky choices and trade-offs that must be made in the world of insurgent warfare.

Immersive Learning Summary

Immersive learning requires active attention, the ability to listen and filter, and to see patterns while staying centered—even when overwhelmed with stimuli. Leaders can't absorb everything, so they must filter out extraneous information and learn how to recognize patterns as they are emerging. The difficulties of signal/noise filtering are increasing dramatically as data sources multiply. Generational differences will be apparent, and leaders who have grown up in the digital age will have better skills for continuous partial attention.

Another requirement for immersive learning ability is an open mindedness beyond what many top executives can muster. Once leaders get toward the top of organizations, even open and informal ones, they get more and more insulated from what is really going on. Leaders need to step outside their protected roles to step inside very different experiences from which they can learn. Ideally, the immersive learning environment will be more difficult than what the leader experiences in the real world. Leaders should seek out immersive learning opportunities—especially experiences that make them uncomfortable in constructive ways.

5

Bio-Empathy

Ability to see things from nature's point of view;
to understand, respect, and learn from nature's patterns.

A significant part of the pleasure of eating is
in one's accurate consciousness of the lives
and the world from which the food comes.
WENDELL BERRY

EATING IS EVERYONE'S everyday link with nature. If we eat
with consciousness about where our food comes from, we have the
potential to empathize more deeply with natural processes. Eating
with awareness is one form of bio-empathy, the ability to learn from
nature. It applies to many different forms of leadership in many dif-

ferent ways. Bio-empathy looks at leadership through a natural filter, in search of the underlying biology of each choice. What are the
underlying patterns of nature that could inform how leaders lead?
Nature teaches, if only we humans can understand its lessons.

In Virginia's Shenandoah Valley, three generations of the Salatin
family have run Polyface Farm since 1961 using the following principles, which do a great job of expressing bio-empathy in practice:[1]

- **Transparency:** Anyone is welcome to visit the farm anytime.
  No trade secrets, no locked doors, every corner is camera-
  accessible.

- **Grass-based:** Pastured livestock and poultry, moved frequently to new "salad bars," offer landscape healing and
  nutritional superiority.[2]

- **Individuality:** Plants and animals should be provided a habitat
  that allows them to express their physiological distinctiveness.
  Respecting and honoring the "pigness" of the pig is a
  foundation for societal health.

- **Community:** We do not ship food. We should all seek food
  closer to home, in our food shed, our own bioregion. This
  means enjoying seasonality and reacquainting ourselves with
  our home kitchens.

- **Nature's template:** Mimicking natural patterns on a commercial domestic scale ensures moral and ethical boundaries
  to human cleverness. Cows are herbivores, not omnivores; that
  is why we've never fed them dead cows like the United States
  Department of Agriculture encouraged (the alleged cause of
  mad cows).

- **Earthworms:** We're really in the earthworm enhancement
  business. Stimulating soil biota is our first priority. Soil health
  creates healthy food.

These are not rules; they are principles. The name of the farm
comes from the practice of polyculture, which is growing two or
more crops on the same piece of land. The Salatins are makers dedi-

cated to farming the perennial prairie on which they live in a way that mimics nature.

They use unique temporary fencing structures that allow the animals to move around the farm, so that other animals can follow them in cycle and do what they do best. Essentially they put them in the context of a farm governed by natural principles and empathy for nature. They have lowered their purchased food dramatically and, by rotating the grazing areas, various animal species play varied natural roles. They are able to work with nature to produce very tasty, very healthy products.

Another kind of bio-empathy is demonstrated by Scott Dye, the orthopedist who had his knee cut open without anesthetic in order to understand knee pain (see chapter 4). Many orthopedists seem to view knee pain as a mechanical problem. Their typical fix is to "replace" the knee. Mechanical knees are impressive, but not nearly as impressive as the real thing. An artificial knee can't really do all the same things in the same way; rather, it provides a limited functional alternative to the natural knee.

Dr. Dye has a different way of thinking: he thinks about the knee biologically, not mechanically, and focuses on knee pain. "From this new biologic perspective, it clinically matters little what structural factors may be present in a given joint . . . if the pain-free condition of tissue homeostasis is safely achieved and maintained."[3] What he learned under the knife led him to a much greater empathy for his patients, but also an appreciation for the amazing design and wonder of the human knee. He does not decide too soon and doesn't rebuild the knee—unless all the other approaches fail. This approach to medical leadership can also be applied to many other forms of leadership, using biology as a source of insight.

The term bio-empathy may take some readers over their California threshold for new-age fluff, but I hope you will bear with me. I'm convinced that the next big economic driver will come from biology and the life sciences. Much of that economic energy will be applied to the global health economy—which not only includes caring for the ill, but also health and wellness. Engineering and control-oriented thinking have merits and will still be important in some quarters, particularly in mature markets with stable technologies where control is possible. The next big wave of change, however, will grow from biological and organic ways of thinking. Bio-empathy is simply the attempt by leaders to stay in touch with and learn from the natural cycles that are all around us. How would your business decisions change if you looked at your company as an ecosystem?

Bio-empathy involves sensitivity to the natural cycles of life, which comes easily to a life scientist; but one can learn it through wilderness camping or just being out in nature. Familiarity with the outdoors and with outdoor living is a big plus for bio-empathy skill building.

The Presiding Bishop of the Episcopal Church, Katharine Jefferts Schori, is another example of a person with bio-empathy, in a very different field from Scott Dye. Before she was ordained, the bishop was an oceanographer for the National Marine Fisheries Service. In addition, she was a science teacher and researcher at Oregon State University. She has spoken from the pulpit about her personal tendency to demand scientific evidence before believing the truth of anything, while at the same time acknowledging areas of mystery, of the unknown. Also a pilot, Bishop Schori uses examples in her teaching and preaching about the power of the wind or spirit, comparing it to Hebrew Scriptures and the New Testament. She often uses biological metaphors in conversation. To promote environmentalism and social justice, she explains the connectivity of everything:

> Scientists are teaching us that everything in the universe is connected, not just complex human and mechanical systems. A remarkable experiment a number of years ago showed this in a new way. If you take a pair of electrons with opposite spins, and send them off in different directions, and then change the spin of one of them, the spin of the other also changes—instantaneously. We're beginning to understand that everything in the universe is connected, even at the most elemental level.[4]

Bishop Schori challenges people to examine the rhythms and tendencies in nature, and to look for resonances in their own lives.

Bio-empathy Defined

Bio-empathy requires seeing things from nature's point of view. Respect for nature is basic to this perspective, with a long-term view of what is needed for life to go on for generations beyond the present. Bio-empathy also depends upon a knack for natural thinking and a leadership resilience that draws from nature's ways.

One characteristic of bio-empathy is being able to see the big picture of ecological systems, not just the components. Some people begin to understand ecosystems through immersion in the natural world by camping or going on a safari. Even in the everyday business world, leaders are often challenged by multiple interrelated variables, nonlinear relationships, and a change cycle that seems to have a life of its own. Every component may be playing an integral part, and the whole system needs adaptability and resilience.

Also, bio-empathy is not *just* seeing things from nature's point of view. You don't need to escape from corporate capitalism and return to the natural world to have strong bio-empathy. Bio-empathy is about seeing human activity as nested within environmental stability and vice versa. Our human systems live within natural systems. Bio-empathy is about respecting the inevitable ecological consequences of one's actions and seeing these new parameters not as barriers but as opportunities. To acquire bio-empathy, one needs to be humble and realize that getting in sync with the processes of nature can add greatly to life.

Biomimicry is one example, where principles of nature get built into products. Some buildings in Africa, for example, are designed around the airflow principles of a termite mound and therefore have less need for air conditioning. Energy efficiency can be improved when it is based on models from nature. Bio-empathy can be a platform for long-term strategic planning, capturing a growing consumer market and opening one's mind to new insights.

Bio-empathy in the Future

In the background visual on the Ten-Year Forecast map inside the book jacket is a natural pattern of cells to demonstrate how nature will always be in the background. However, the issues of nature—both challenges and opportunities—will come to the foreground over the next decade. Biology and the life sciences will become the critical driver of business performance. Gradually, humans are facing up to their part in abusing the earth and are sincerely looking for ways to make things better from nature's point of view. The dilemma is how to get greener while allowing corporations to make money and be sustainable along with the environment.

BIO-EMPATHY AS THE BASIS FOR INDUSTRY COLLABORATION

The Global Environmental Management Initiative (GEMI) is an industry association for environmental, health, and safety leaders in a wide range of organizations across industries. GEMI worked with Institute for the Future to do a forecast of external future forces affecting sustainability. The forecast map we created looks at sustainability through seven different lenses: people, regions, built environments, nature, markets, business, and energy.[5] With so much activity around it right now, even the term "sustainability" has come to be used in many different ways. The starting place for GEMI was to sort out the various options and put them all on one page for comparison, looking across functions and across industries.

This kind of forecasting is useful because it maps the territory of external future forces. Like any map, the GEMI/IFTF forecast map does not tell people where to go, but it does provide a context for leadership in sustainability. Organizations and individual leaders can place themselves in the stories of the map and consider their roles in the context of the external future forces. The forecast map gives leaders a big-picture typology of the options and the forces that they are likely to encounter on the way to their goal.

GEMI leaders tend to be focused on the technical aspects of environment, health, and safety. Sustainability has now been elevated to a topic for discussion at the most senior levels of a firm. The GEMI map gives a framework for these conversations, as well as some specific suggestions of hot zones where organizations can have the biggest impacts.

IFTF is also working with Business for Social Responsibility (BSR)

FIGURE 11. GEMI map. *Source:* IFTF, Map of Future
Forces Affecting Sustainability, 2007. SR# 1073.

to create a series of cross-industry scenarios to explore how sustainability concern and business strategy can be brought together in creative ways. There are many new models for business strategy that incorporate concern for sustainability, but there is a lot to learn and the pressures to learn are urgent. Bio-empathy must be expressed in business models that are economically sustainable as well as good for the environment.

BIO-EMPATHY AND WARFARE

The families of soldiers serving in Iraq are learning from immersion experiences in nature to help them cope with the side effects of war. Operation Purple is a camp for kids of soldiers who are in Iraq. Sponsored by the Sierra Club, the entire premise of the camp is built on healing through nature. This camping experience is a "leap away from the worries of war."[6] The kids learn how to work through stressful challenges in a low-risk and supportive environment with others who are going through the same things. These children get to see, touch, and feel the military equipment that their parents are using in Iraq. For example, they feel how heavy a bulletproof vest really is, so they have the sense that their parents do have *some* protection. They practice finding adults they can turn to when their parents are not there or not able to help and also build their own resilience in a natural outdoor setting.[7]

ECOSYSTEM EMPATHY

Ecosystems are lives in balance, at least on the good days when they *are* in balance. Ecosystems are not problems to be solved or machines that can be controlled; they are life systems that need to be nurtured as delicate dilemmas of life.

Over the next decade, the issues that are likely to dominate are food, energy, and water, or FEW, as they are coming to be called.[8] All three of them interrelate and all are laced with dilemmas.

There is great potential here to flip these dilemmas into new ways of thinking about priorities. For example, I was speaking recently at the University of Texas business school in Austin as part of a course called "Marketing for Social Profit." That is an interesting flip, where "profit" is applied much more broadly but is still very much within the tradition of the profit motive.[9] Social profit is economic return that also includes positive social impacts and usually involves creating shared assets.

What we call the "Blue Economy" on the Ten-Year Forecast map symbolizes water, which will be the focal point of economic development and environmental debate as we struggle with collapsing fisheries, search for new energy sources, and attempt to manage the impacts of global climate change. Some of these shared resources have finite limits, which are already stretched. Other resources can be stretched with new technology and shared for greater benefits. Ecosystems present many dilemmas, in many different forms. These eco-dilemmas can lead to insight regarding specific innovation opportunities and engagement.

Oceans are shared; no country, region, or person really owns them, yet all of us depend on them. The tidal zones, where land meets ocean, will be a battleground for dilemmas over the next decade, dilemmas that are likely to become even worse in twenty to forty years. Compass (the Communication Partnership for Science and the Sea), for example, is a collaborative effort by scientists to bridge the fields of marine conservation, public interest, and marine policy. Their mission is to accelerate the pace of dilemma flipping within the context of the challenges that they face. They start with a deep empathy for oceans and the value they provide.

BIO-EMPATHY AND FOOD

Created in 2000 as part of a merger, Syngenta is an agribusiness that has reframed its vision and its business as sustainable agriculture. Their focus is on plants, both seeds and crop protection. Growers of all kinds are their customers.

Syngenta has a very clear vision statement that is infused with bio-empathy: "We bring plant potential to life." This is a natural statement of future intent with bio-empathy and an aspiration built in. Notice how they frame their Winning Proposition in the context of external future forces:

> Over the next twenty years, the world's population will rise by about another two billion. Calorie demand will grow even faster, as diets in countries such as China increasingly shift to meat.
>
> In much of the world, agricultural land is limited and water scarce. So tomorrow's growers will have to produce much more food and animal feed with today's natural resources. At the same time, they will continue growing fibers like cotton, and add crops for fuels such as bioethanol. And agriculture also has to protect the environment, for example, by reducing greenhouse gases and preserving natural habitats from the plow.
>
> This all means that growers must increase their yields—the amount of crop per field. Our products play a key role in making that possible.
>
> Bringing plant potential to life.[10]

Syngenta is using its own version of bio-empathy to address the challenges of food production, using science focused on plants. It is creating a business in the midst of the food web. So far, this seems to be working very well for the company and for its customers.

Food dilemmas will proliferate over the next decade and will reflect the rich/poor gap most dramatically. Even as many are hungry, some will be extremely and exotically well fed. Nobody knows how to solve this dilemma, but many leaders will figure out creative ways to flip this situation and make it better. In just the last few years, concepts like the "100-mile Diet" and "locavores" (a word that designates those who eat only local foods) have become popular and—in at least some locations in some seasons—practical. Although some of the current focus on locally grown food could be a fad, the interest is indicative of deeper concerns about food sourcing. People want to know that their food is safe, and it seems safer if it is local or if they know where it comes from. People also want to consume less energy, and local food does not need to be transported.

In the world of the future, food chains are giving way to webs. Linear and mechanical procedures for distributing food are being replaced by cyclical, organic, flexible food webs. Food webs are the complex, interlocking, and interdependent feeding relationships among plant and animal species. Food companies traditionally used "supply chains" to distribute food for sale. In most corporations these chains are now referred to as "supply networks" or "supply webs." These webs will be challenged by global climate change, overdevelopment, and industrial waste, but they are also more robust than ever.

Over the next decade, leaders can expect a confusing mix of choices with regard to food, distribution, and transparency. As ecologist Daniel Janzen says, "It's all gardening now."[11] Gardening requires bio-empathy.

BIO-EMPATHY AT THE BALLPARK

Scott Jenkins is an example of a business leader with strong bio-empathy. Jenkins is the head of ballpark operations at Safeco Field, where the Seattle Mariners play major league baseball. He was

FIGURES 12 & 13 (right and opposite). Captain Plastic is a family-friendly voice of sustainability at Safeco Field. He teaches kids to recycle as part of the family experience at the park. *Source:* Used with permission of Ben VanHouten, photographer.

trained in construction management at the University of Wisconsin, with courses in environmental studies as well. Basically he is an outdoors person who spent a lot of time running along the shore of Lake Michigan when he was a kid in Kenosha. Jenkins has gained a reputation as a kind of "Mr. Green Stadium" for his work on the greening of stadiums for the Milwaukee Brewers, the Philadelphia Eagles, and now the Seattle Mariners. He has limited formal training in environmental sustainability, but he has lots of interest to learn and lots of passion for the challenges. He was not taught bio-empathy in his formal course work, but he lives it.

Safeco Field is the stadium that I find most like Walt Disney World in terms of its family friendliness. If you use a four-letter word there, you will get warned once and then escorted quietly out of the park. The rule of thumb is that behavior must be appropriate in the company of a seven-year-old. The Safeco Field Code of Conduct is displayed around the park and if you violate it, you get a red card that includes the following warning: "The Safeco Field Code of Conduct asks all of our guests to respect others around them by avoiding foul or abusive language, obscene gestures, and other abusive behavior. *If you receive this card, we believe that your behavior has crossed this line.* Please

take this as a friendly reminder. Enjoy the game, but allow others to do so as well. Continued abusive behavior will require us to eject you from the ballpark without refund—something we don't want to do."

Part of being family friendly, according to Scott Jenkins, is being friendly to the environment. Bio-empathy relates to people as much as it does to plants and animals. Jenkins was hired to be the Vice President of Ballpark Operations, but he brought his bio-empathy with him. When he came to Safeco Field, Jenkins asked his staff (it takes about 2,000 people to put on a single event at this stadium) how much energy it took to run the entire stadium for one day. Nobody actually knew at the time (including Scott), but they know now. Jenkins has put in feedback systems that let people know how much energy they are using and gives them rewards for saving energy. Safeco Field is looking for ways to give real-time feedback to its own employees (called team members) and to its fans.

Jenkins has great focus on the direction he is going as he greens Safeco Field while also improving the family experience, but he realizes that there are lots of steps along the way and many behaviors that must be changed. Jenkins himself bikes to and from the ballpark. His first car was the Honda CRX HF, one of the first hybrids, which averaged fifty to sixty miles per gallon, and he now drives a Prius using hyper-mileage driving principles. (He told me that when he drives his car, he goes "as slow as I can without annoying people.") When I walked with Scott Jenkins around the stadium, he always stopped to pick up paper on the ground or clean any spills. He teaches everyone to take responsibility for the cleanliness of the park, which is a discipline that people at Disney follow as well.

One kind of feedback that Safeco team members get is from secret shoppers. The Mariners hire shoppers (disguised as normal fans, some with kids) to attend every game and give specific feedback about how they were treated and what they experienced. The feedback is not used in an evaluative way, but rather as a way to encourage staff to behave in a manner that is family friendly and green. The Mariners G.A.M.E. Plan is this clear statement of intent:

- **G**uests come first.
- **A**ttitude is everything.
- **M**ake memories.
- **E**veryone is empowered.

Staff members are rewarded around these principles and given encouragement about ways to improve. The secret shoppers are looking for behavior that I would call bio-empathy, especially empathy for the biological units called baseball fans.

The Mariners use the secret shoppers in a way that is reminiscent of the army and other public service agencies using After Action Reviews. The Mariners' "make memories" principle is similar to the way in which Walt Disney World park workers are encouraged to create magical experiences for the guests. They are not looking for someone to blame; they are looking for ways to give quick feedback on positive behavior that supports the overall fan experience they are trying to create. This is very motivational for the employees, since they get both the fulfillment of creating memories for the fans and also the quick feedback on their level of friendliness at the ballpark.

Bio-empathy gets played out within the context of the family-friendly vision and strategy for Safeco Field. Energy-saving behavior increased dramatically when employees were taught how they could save energy and given immediate feedback when they did. Much of the savings has come through behavior changes and creating a different set of disciplines at work. Team members are encouraged to treat the ballpark as they would their own home, as if they were paying the utility bills.

Changes in products and processes have helped as well. Safeco Field now uses bottle-shaped recycling containers that are message-branded with their own "Captain Plastic" logo and positioned all around the park with requests for people to "Join the Green Team." The drinking cups for beer and soft drinks are not petroleum based and can be recycled, for example. The systemic changes, however, were all done in the context of behavior, and the behavior changes were done in the context of the family-friendly spirit of Safeco Field. This version of bio-empathy begins with the family—especially the kids. In Seattle's ballpark, family friendly is bio-friendly.

BIO-EMPATHY IN A POPULAR TV SHOW

Cesar Milan is the star of the very successful *National Geographic* TV series called *The Dog Whisperer*. His mantra is "I rehabilitate dogs, I train humans." Certainly, Milan is a showman who has created a great story around himself and his presence with dogs. Behind the drama and the considerable hype, there are some basic principles that express strong positive bio-empathy toward dogs and people. He is facilitating cross-species communication and is a maker of new relationships between dogs and humans, following his own maker instinct and bio-empathy.

Milan has great bio-empathy with dogs. (He's lived with them all of his life, beginning on a farm in Mexico where he was born.) His experience led him to a basic insight about what dogs want and need: exercise, discipline, and affection, in that order. This statement is a wonderful example of expressing intent with great clarity, but still with flexibility regarding how the exercise, discipline, and affection are delivered. I find his insight useful in my own life, not only with dogs, but also in my understanding of myself and other people. All of us need exercise, discipline, and affection—though not necessarily in that order. Dogs, however, are different from humans in important ways that humans often forget in their efforts to cuddle and care for them.

With a commander's intent and a strong presence with dogs, Milan's calm assertive energy, indeed his entire body positioning, shows strong clarity. He allows dogs to be themselves, but only within prescribed parameters. He doesn't train dogs; he rehabilitates them. He trains humans to have the same kind of bio-empathy with dogs that he has. People working with dogs should ask: what energy am I communicating? Certainly, every leader should also ask this question. Milan argues that a leader's energy must be calm and assertive—not nervous energy. I suspect that applies to human leaders as well.

Cesar Milan coaches dog owners to learn that when they fail, which we all do, they have to focus on what they really want and stay focused through failure on to the next challenge. A lot of energy gets pent up around defeats. Dogs live in the moment and start over again with each new experience. Dogs may be easily upset, but they can come into a balanced state of mind. Doesn't this sound similar to leaders immersing themselves in the VUCA world and coming up with a way to win anyway? Perhaps it is easier to understand the future by beginning with the challenges of understanding how to work across species between a human and a dog. It is also important, of course, not to generalize too casually from dogs to humans. Milan tells a funny story about his wife's sharp reminder to him that she does not respond to exercise, discipline, and affection—in that order.

Bio-empathy Summary

A leader should reflect (as water reflects) nature. There are many ways to develop bio-empathy, but the first step is to observe and appreciate the natural processes that are always going on around you. Bio-empathy contributes to person-to-person communication. Mimicking natural processes ensures moral and ethical boundaries for human action. Every organization's guiding principles should reflect bio-empathy and express it in organic—not mechanical—language. Bio-empathy takes big-picture thinking that respects all the multiple interrelated parts and nonlinear relationships, as well as cycles of change.

Bio-empathy is grounded in an ability to empathize with nature and understand its ways, its connectivity, and its resilience. One interesting strategy is to learn about science and nature through children's books, such as those published by Dorling Kindersley.[12] If you don't have a background in science or outdoor living, it is not too late to learn.

6

Constructive Depolarizing

Ability to calm tense situations

where differences dominate and communication has broken down—

and bring people from divergent cultures

toward constructive engagement.

NEUROLOGIST ROBERT BURTON is studying the neuroscience of certainty. He has conclusions that will influence the future of leadership, including the premise of his new book, *On Being Certain: Believing You Are Right Even When You're Not:*

> Despite how certainty feels, it is neither a conscious choice nor even a thought process. Certainty and similar states of 'knowing we know' arise out of involuntary brain mechanisms that, like love and anger, function independently of reason.[1]

I believe that the quest for certainty will increase over the next decade because people will have a need to be certain in uncertain times. Nobody has created a VUCA index to measure just how volatile, uncertain, complex, and ambiguous our time is as compared to previous times in history. That would be interesting, but I'm not sure how useful it would be. The important point is how leaders perceive the context around them. What do they expect? Expectations will be key in shaping what leaders think is possible. I believe that the future will be more VUCA than what most of the world is experiencing today, and I think it's safest for leaders to assume this also. Whether this is the case, however, is less important than the fact that VUCA will abound. Leaders need to learn how to lead in an extremely uncertain age, perhaps the most uncertain that any generation of leaders has yet had to face.

The more uncertainty there is in the external world, the more people will need to feel certain—or at least assured. Religious, political, social, and psychological fundamentalism will increase in an attempt to reel in the chaos of the external world. The neuroscience of certainty is likely to become an important field of study, along with other attempts to make sense out of certainty.

In these times, many different groups will believe that they are right; some of those will believe that everyone else is wrong. Leaders will need to engage with extreme groups who may not even agree with other similar groups. Extreme positions and polarization will be commonplace. Engaging with those who are obsessed with certainty—whatever the source—will be difficult indeed.

In polarized situations, differences are sharply drawn and communication has disintegrated. In a chaotic world, there are often more than two points of view and there are usually many stakeholders. Constructive depolarization is a skill that all leaders will need. Leaders need to redirect the energy of conflict and bring the stakeholders toward constructive engagement and dialogue.

In times of change, simplified certainty will lure those who are most confused. The next decade will be characterized by extreme reactions to the VUCA world and its chaos. When people go over their own personal threshold of disruption, they will seek easy and quick solutions. If the uncertainty is too great for a particular individual, certainty is a logical psychological reaction. It may also be a neurological demand. Certainty is a response not only to uncertainty in the external world, but to inner needs as well. Leaders will need to show a sense of confidence and appropriate certainty, while still having caution about too much or false certainty.

Constructive Depolarization Defined

Constructive depolarization is the maker instinct applied to a conflict, an attempt to remake polarization into dialogue. When leaders encounter conflict, the temptation is to pick sides. Picking sides, however, is rarely a good strategy. Conflicts are often dilemmas that must be flipped in order to make good progress. The story of constructive depolarization is usually a drama, with many twists in the plot.

A background in cultural anthropology (ethnography), qualitative sociology (participant observation), or comparative religions will be very helpful for future leaders. International travel and living in a variety of places can be very instructive, as can language skills. Thomas Friedman's argument that the "world is flat" is true in one sense, but the world is also extremely diverse—with many varying cultural characteristics, religious beliefs, and economic pressures. The more comfortable a leader is with cultural diversity, the more likely he or she is to be able to lead in diverse organizations.

Future leaders will need cross-cultural grace in order to constructively depolarize a situation: an ability to listen and learn from people who are very different from them, and perhaps different in a disturbing way. Grace in this sense means being nimble, poised, and smooth—like a good dancer. It is the ability to offer consideration and respect whether or not a person deserves it. Leaders with grace will be able to make the reconciliation process look easy. In exploring this critical future leadership skill, I turned back to the iconic anthropologist E.T. Hall, author of *The Silent Language: An Anthropologist Reveals How We Communicate by Our Manners and Behavior.* Hall argues that culture is communication and communication is culture. The "silent language" of culture will always be hidden, but Hall gives leaders some useful advice: ". . . we must learn to understand the 'out of awareness' aspects of communication. We must never assume that we are fully aware of what we communicate to someone else."[2]

Hall worked for the State Department helping diplomatic leaders understand and learn from other cultures. Cross-cultural leadership is now much more complex than it was when Hall published *The Silent Language*. Cross-cultural does not just refer to ethnic, national, and regional beliefs. Leaders must take into account age, gender, disabilities, and other dimensions of difference. There are many cultures and subcultures, and the web allows dispersed cultures to connect and influence each other—for better or worse. Polarization is most likely to occur between different cultures. Constructive depolarization is about grace across barriers of culture, nationality, or ethnicity.

Dilemmas in the Future

The next decade will be characterized by diversity and polarization, much of which will trace its roots to the growing and increasingly visible gap between the rich and the poor. One aspect of the gap is narrowing, however: even poor people are gaining access to cheap digital meeting tools that can be used for organizing. In general, extreme groups tend to be better at web organizing, which means that even very small extreme groups could have major impacts far beyond their numbers. Cheap ubiquitous cell phones, for example, can bring cohorts of people together and give voice to their concerns.

In ten years it is clear that pretty much everything will have a global and cross-cultural aspect—our differences will be visible to everyone. It will be rare to find situations that are exclusively local, simple, and homogeneous. For example, Wayne Sensor, the CEO of Alegent Health in Omaha, Nebraska, came to IFTF to talk about Alegent's work on global health. When I asked why a local health care provider that only serves the inland state of Nebraska would be so interested in global health issues, he responded, "Because planes fly into Omaha." Indeed, air travel increases the very real possibility of pandemics. Local organizations often have global suppliers, even if all employees are not aware of how globally connected they really are. Global issues will profoundly affect people who have previously seen themselves as operating on a local level. Food safety in China may seem like it is a far-away issue, until you realize that some of the ingredients in your "local" food products came from China and may have been tainted.

POLARITIES IN FAITH

The Consortium of Endowed Episcopal Parishes (CEEP) is made up of U.S.-based Episcopal churches, which are part of the global Anglican Communion, which is one of the largest social networks in the world; it is a diaspora, with strong links based on values in spite of its great diversity of members.

The U.S. Episcopal Church is immersed in controversy over the ordination of gay bishops, which brings to the surface issues of authority within this diffuse global network. The debate over whether gay people should be ordained as bishops raises basic theological, psychological, and sexual questions that are difficult to discuss without emotion—sometimes extreme emotion. The situation is so polarized that dialogue is often impossible.

The Consortium asked IFTF to do an independent forecast of external future forces that will be important for Episcopal congregations to consider in the next ten years. Figure 14 shows the modified Foresight to Insight to Action Cycle that we created as part of this forecast, which we called *The Book of Provocation,* a conscious play on the Bible's Book of Revelation. Our forecast was designed to stimulate conversations among church members not only about present conflicts, but about what they have in common as they think about the future. The case is still out as to whether or not we will succeed, but there are parishes around the United States using *The Book of Provocation* to spark conversations among people of faith.

I believe that forecasting has the power to bring people together for dialogue across polarities, if they can step back as they look ahead.

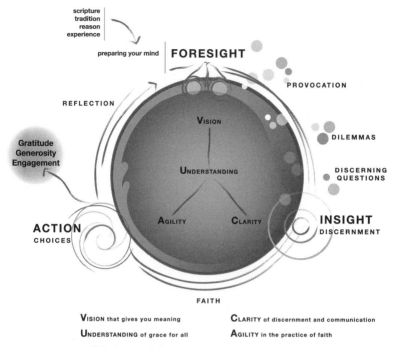

FIGURE 14. Modified Foresight to Insight to Action cycle for *The Book of Provocation. Source:* IFTF, *The Book of Provocation: Faith in the Future Conversations,* 2008. SR# 1123.

It is necessary, however, to find an internal logic in this kind of situation. In the Anglican Communion, there is a great history of openness and engagement. Starting from scripture, reason, and tradition, a Ten-Year Forecast of external future forces can provide a context for faith communities. The forecast, however, is not a prediction of the future. That future, we hope, will be shaped by people in the local congregations who become inspired by "Faith in the Future Conversations," as we are calling them.

Every ten years, the global Anglican Communion holds a nineteenday summit for bishops. In the summer of 2008 the Lambeth Conference was held at the University of Kent in Canterbury. The polarizing issue on everyone's mind was the ordination of gay bishops. The one openly gay bishop, Bishop Gene Robinson from New Hampshire, was not invited to attend, but he was given space to meet with bishops from around the world as part of what was known as the "fringe" event. One hundred and fifty bishops decided not to attend the conference out of protest against the ordination of gay bishops.

This conference focused on person-to-person engagement and constructive depolarization. While the threat of a split church loomed, the goal of the conference was to honor the participants and their varied approaches to faith, so that the bishops from around the world could get to know each other as people—not polarities. They were trying to lay the groundwork for engagement with diversity, following principles which were not only Anglican, but also good for anyone trying to constructively depolarize a conflict.

The conference employed an African Zulu method called *Indaba*, used to allow villagers to meet and discuss problems in the community. In hopes that the Bible could provide a common starting ground, the conference began with Bible study groups of eight randomly assigned people reading the "I am" statements in the Gospel of John, as chosen by the Archbishop of Canterbury. Then groups of eight joined together to create assemblages of forty bishops, with an "animateur" to get things started and facilitate, a "rapporteur" to take notes, and a listener, who summarized.

These evolving groups put an emphasis on personal contact among the participants, rather than pushing through ideas or positions. While the *Indaba* methods seem similar to Western approaches, I expect that its African origin contributed to the sense of constructive engagement between developed and emerging economies. The African bishops felt most outcast going in, but the use of a process that was familiar to them perhaps gave them a sense of trust that they would not have had otherwise. Canon Gregory Cameron, one of the chief mediators, summarized the challenges:

> No organization exists without internal conflict—not even the church. What is important is that organizations achieve enough unity to continue to fulfill their purposes. Our challenge is harnessing that which is best in the life of the church so that we have something to say not just to ourselves but to the world.[3]

The goal of the conference was to hold the Anglican Communion together as a network, while allowing space for individual self-expression. The group process encouraged the participants to hold off on making judgments too early. Of course, many of the participants had strong views before they arrived, but this conference opening created a time to reflect and reconsider as the participants got to know each other as people.

The Lambeth Conference illustrates the polarized engagement we are all likely to experience in the next decade. The quality of the outcome from Lambeth is debatable, but at least the bishops engaged in thoughtful conversation.

CIVIC ENGAGEMENT ACROSS POLARITIES

The technologies of cooperation are getting much better, and they will be able to help us bridge polarities and deal with controversial issues. One of the pioneers of computer support for large-scale meetings is Lenny Lind, who founded CoVision in 1985. The company mantra is "Building collective intelligence through high-engagement meetings." CoVision facilitates large in-person meetings by distributing laptops around the room to allow for instant polling and participation from more individuals than would be possible using conventional means. Trained facilitators solicit wide input and help the participants sort out common concerns, as well as create an action agenda. They use interactive panels through the electronic media to allow more voices to be heard.

For example, in 2005 CoVision worked with AmericaSpeaks to gather one thousand people in a large room for the Clinton Global Initiative in New York. The focus was on four parallel tracks: energy and climate, global health, poverty alleviation, and mitigating religious and ethnic conflict. Former president Bill Clinton was the chair. World leaders were joined by senior government officials, public and private infrastructure experts, celebrities, business leaders, billionaires, philanthropists, and other notables—all sitting at round tables discussing the most important problems facing the world community.

It was a marketplace of ideas and initiatives. The meeting was origi-
nally conceived of as a "world economic forum with an action plan."
Indeed, hundreds of specific commitments to action were made and
millions of dollars were raised. The process is continuing beyond this
single event.

The electronic tools for civic engagement are getting much better, as are the processes for using the technology effectively. Over
the next ten years, I expect that electronically assisted group processes like this will become more common in civic engagement.
These media allow conversations that bridge polarities, using ano-
nymity and simultaneous exchange in ways that are not possible in
traditional face-to-face meetings. In this way, diverse groups can be
brought together for constructive depolarization and engagement.

POLARITIES OF WAR

At one of our civilian/military workshops at the Army War College,
I asked two strategy professors, one from Columbia Business School
and one from the Army War College, to prepare an introductory lec-
ture on strategy. About an hour before they went on, I asked them to
exchange PowerPoints and use each other's slides for their introductory lectures. Then, I facilitated a panel discussion that compared
strategy in business to the way it is practiced in the military.

There were many similarities in the basic concepts and principles. For example, Commander's Intent is basic to military strategy
and it is quite similar to a Winning Proposition or strategic intent
in the corporate world. What's different is that military strategy is
much more complicated than business strategy. There are so many
variables and so many stakeholders. In addition to the complexity of
military strategy, war has life and death consequences.

If a military conflict involves religious beliefs, things get even
messier. I've been very impressed in recent years with the approach
coming to be called "faith-based diplomacy."[4] In traditional media-
tion, religion was considered out of bounds and the effort was toward
a secular resolution. In faith-based diplomacy, religious representatives on both sides of the polarization get involved and share the

precepts from each faith that speak to forgiveness and reconciliation. They look for common ground on which both sides can build. Of course, the introduction of faith adds even further to the complexity of the strategy discussion, but it is also closer to areas where lasting agreements might be achieved.

Thus, constructive depolarization is much more difficult in a military setting—especially if life-and-death decisions are involved. Leaders need a strategy for engagement and exploration, but they also need diplomatic skills that go far beyond the fighting and well into peacekeeping and even nation building. I met a young man recently who had just returned from Iraq, where one of his tasks had been walking door to door to introduce the concept of democracy. Think of that. Certainly, his military training did not prepare him for this, but that is what he had to do. This very human door-to-door process was critical to American attempts (many would say failed attempts) to depolarize a very bad situation and try to make it better. This young man was trying to be an agent of constructive depolarization. When I met him, he was reading the Koran in an attempt to understand the people he was meeting. The human contact may not have outweighed the negatives of the military tactics, but it certainly put forward a different approach to engagement that attempted to diffuse a very tense situation.

NEW POLARITIES OF NORMALCY

One of the big polarities in our society today is between people who are classified as "normal" and those who are not. People with disabilities have been marginalized by our society and by our policies toward them. Products, services, and technologies designed for people with disabilities have been treated as a do-good activity, if there has been any market activity at all. Public policy toward people with disabilities has been more or less stalled for the last decade, without much effort to constructively depolarize and build new definitions of normality. People with disabilities are likely to feel this polarization deeply.

The next decade will see some big changes in notions of normality.

One of the few positive results of the Iraq War is the incredible effort in medical technology to rebuild broken bodies. Indeed, technology has evolved to the point where "normal" may just be a temporary zone on the way to becoming better than normal. New drugs, for example, are likely to amplify leadership abilities by allowing people to stay awake and alert longer. People who can afford it will be able to understand their own genomic profiles so they can take better care of their bodies.

People with disabilities are the earlier explorers of this future world, and since they already experience their own challenges of volatility, uncertainty, complexity, and ambiguity, they may in fact be more ready for the VUCA world than those who are "not yet disabled," as they sometimes refer to the rest of the world. The true innovations are likely to come from the margins that are stretched, rather than from the mainstream.

CONSTRUCTIVE DEPOLARIZATION VIA YOUTUBE

In a BBC World News interview, Queen Rania of Jordan said, "Violence has overtaken dialogue, and compassion has lost out to anger. I'm hoping this will become a channel of communication between East and West because I very much think our world is in dire need of that . . . As Muslims we need to stand up and speak out about who we are. If we want to defy stereotypes we have to start defining ourselves, and we're not going to do that just by sitting quietly at home expecting people to just get it."[5] Constructive depolarization involves both deep self-knowledge and the ability to communicate effectively across differences, using media appropriate to the task.

As Queen Rania pointed out, the Islamic faith is made up of many different diasporas with many different beliefs and practices. From the outside, Islam can look much more monolithic than it really is. What looks like one diaspora is actually several, all loosely connected in the traditions of Islam. Stereotypes are dangerous because they oversimplify, and sometimes in ways that provoke extreme reactions.

In 2008, Queen Rania began using YouTube to present her own video log with a goal of clarifying Islamic beliefs and Muslim tradi-

FIGURE 15. Jordan's Queen Rania has a video log on YouTube clarifying Islamic beliefs and Muslim traditions. *Source:* Used with permission of Ghada Al-Shami.

tions for the rest of the world. She created this site and invited questions and comments.

Nobody yet knows the full impacts of Queen Rania's efforts, but they are certainly inspirational in their use of new media to constructively depolarize tensions between the people of Islam and the rest of the world.

Constructive Depolarization Summary

Mentoring is great, but reverse-mentoring is better. Reverse-mentoring is a simple but powerful strategy for crossing the polarities of the future. Many innovative organizations already have reverse-mentoring programs, and they are of great benefit. For example, young scientists mentor senior executives with no science background; young Facebook users mentor their Boomer managers in social networking skills. Mentors have traditionally been experienced, often older, people who show the ropes to those who are less experienced and younger. In situations where young people are actually more skilled than older people—as is often the case with the new social media— why not reverse this process? Leaders and soon-to-be leaders should look for these opportunities.

Role reversal has always been a basic technique for conflict resolution. The idea is to try to see the world from the other side of an issue. Constructive depolarization starts with an ability to listen deeply and engage with people on all sides of a conflict. We need to seek out our common humanity and empathize with others who come from very different points of view. Calming tense situations, however, is just a beginning. Creating constructive ways forward is much more difficult to sustain. Leaders will need to calm tensions and move through the conflict.

Extreme polarization will be a driving force for the foreseeable future, so leaders will need a personal strategy and style for constructive depolarization that goes beyond picking sides.

7

Quiet Transparency

Ability to be open and authentic
about what matters to you—
without advertising yourself.

THE *MAKE: MAGAZINE* MOTTO, "If you can't open it, you don't own it,"[1] is a call—really a demand—for transparency. Transparency is rooted in the maker instinct. People's curiosity and knowledge about how things are made has always been there, but will increase dramatically. Where did those ingredients come from? What standards of safety were used? How green were the factories? Who were the workers and how were they treated?

New technology, such as sensors everywhere and wireless connectivity, will fuel the growth of transparency—like it or not. Transparency won't be as easy or as even as desirable as it sounds; it will often be problematic. Although increasing transparency is inevitable, definitions of transparency and what is being seen will vary.

Companies and their leaders are being called upon to be transparent at every step of a product's life cycle from birth to death. If they aren't transparent, it is likely that others will make assumptions and create their own definitions of those processes. Transparency is in the eye of the beholder, or the metrics of the person doing the measuring. If you don't measure yourself, you are likely to be measured by others. "Measure or be measured" is likely to be a motto in the future, but "measure *and* be measured" may be more accurate.

For example, many retailers now require a carbon footprint assessment for products they sell. This is a calculation of a product's environmental impact. It means that potential buyers can compare and make decisions informed by the comparison. Although rating the environmental sustainability of a product is a step in the right direction, it is not that simple.

Carbon footprints are not measurable in an absolute sense; they are only calculable. The calculation depends on how far back and how far forward you go in the life cycle of the product you are evaluating. Detergents, for example, have a different carbon footprint in France than they do in the United States because power is generated differently in each country and the key variable is the water temperature at which the detergent is used.

A single carbon footprint number is based upon several assumptions—most of which are never even known by the person making the purchase. In other words, these calculations are debatable. Unfortunately, the difficulties of measuring objectively are likely to get worse over the next decade. These assessments are good to do, but also problematic. It is just one example of how the demand for transparency will grow—even as the calculations become more debatable.

Consumers want a simple measure of environmental impact, and retailers are anxious to give it to them. Manufacturers will often just have to do the best they can in difficult situations. In many cases, companies are likely to provide a simple number for something that is not simple. The good news is that we will have improved transparency. The bad news is that there will be a variety of interpretations. Everyone is just figuring out what transparency really means and, more importantly, what it could mean in the future. Measuring carbon footprints is just one example. Transparency is more a dilemma than a problem, since few things are absolutely transparent in a way that everyone will agree upon.

Quiet Transparency Defined

Quiet transparency in leadership begins with humility. Leaders should be self-effacing and not self-promoting—as well as open. Why are you doing what you are doing? Why does it matter to you? The younger the worker, the more likely he or she is to ask questions like this. The older the manager, the less likely he or she is to be transparent about the answers to these questions. Still, more people will be interested in why leaders do what they do.

Quiet transparency goes beyond traditional command-and-control leadership styles, which operate on the principle that, unless you need to know something, you are not told. In a transparent world, all have access to information—even if they don't have the need. And different people may well have different interpretations of what the transparency reveals because it is rarely absolute.

Whether they are more or less transparent, leaders will definitely have to give up some control. They need to decide what they themselves can and want to manage, since they cannot directly supervise everything. Leadership control is something of an illusion. Most top executives are surprised when they reach the top and learn that they have less power than they'd imagined. In the world of the future, control will rarely be possible.

Some degree of transparency will be required of all leaders, certainly more than in the past. It will still be possible to keep some things private, but they will be limited and defined by your leadership role. Business, government, or nonprofit leaders, for example, may be able to protect their private lives more than politicians or celebrities will. Quiet transparency means that leaders will decide what measures are important to them (and to the people they lead) and then be completely open about those measures—but not necessarily about everything.

The evaluator of transparency, not the person or organization being assessed, usually gets to define what it means. Often, leaders will not get to decide how it is measured, even when they are measuring themselves. If the customer, consumer, or public thinks it is important to be transparent about certain issues, then leaders need to respond appropriately, using measures that others will trust. Quiet transparency requires trust from both the leader and from those who choose to follow. Leaders cannot be transparent if people don't trust them. Transparency implies the measurement is true.

Transparency is also about authenticity, as Joe Pine and Jim Gilmore state in their recent book, *Authenticity*.[2] Pine and Gilmore coined the term "experience economy," which refers to the overall direction of economic evolution: from commodity products to services to experiences to personal transformations. The further you get from products and the closer you get to transformations, the more important authenticity becomes. Leadership authenticity inspires credibility and trust. It also allows followers to see in their leaders not only a bit of themselves but also that which makes them aspire to be more. Quiet transparency does not mix well with fame, celebrity, or acclaim. A leader doesn't need to be a celebrity to be successful, and in some cases, success and recognition may be inversely correlated. Often, the best change agents get no credit for the changes that they seed.

At Institute for the Future, we have found that many popular experts with wide public acclaim are not very good at forecasting. For our expert panels in the early days of IFTF, we would look for the most famous leaders in a particular field. We quickly found, however, that expertise at forecasting does not correlate with celebrity. There are just too many pressures on those who get the most publicity, such as audience demand for the same talk over and over again—for large amounts of money. For our panels, we tend to seek out experts who are either not yet celebrities or do not want to be famous.

People who are used to the spotlight can recede into their own bubbles, often losing not only their ability to forecast, but their ability to make the future. There are certainly exceptions where celebrities are great leaders, but it is a very tricky balance to sustain. Perhaps the most difficult challenge of quiet transparency is to become a great leader without becoming too much of a celebrity. This is certainly a dilemma, since successful leaders will always have to deal with some elements of fame, but they should resist the urge to be stars.

I realize that quiet transparency is not something that all leaders will find attractive. Many leaders still want to be rock stars. They will not see self-promotion as bad, but rather as important in order to get to the top and achieve the fame they desire. I believe that humble strength, however, will win out in the future.

Dilemmas in the Future

Outside scrutiny of leaders is likely to grow in the world of the future as the tools for sensing, measuring, and monitoring—the tools of transparency—become ubiquitous. Also, it seems that there is more to be transparent about and more people who want to know what leaders are doing. In the future, they will have the tools to do it. Measuring devices will be everywhere, connected to people all around the world.

NEW TECHNOLOGY FOR TRANSPARENCY

"Pervasive computing" has been around for many years, but over the next decade it will become practical and truly universal. It is reasonable to expect a world instrumented with sensors, actuators, and information processors integrated with objects, activities, and many aspects of life.

A society that employs pervasive computing will be very different. Many things that are currently invisible will become visible through a vast array of measurement devices that make transparency so much more possible and accessible. Pervasive computing means that transparency will be mandatory in many environments, whether that transparency is "quiet" or not. The leaders of the civic structure and the grassroots actions of the community will set the specific measures of the transparency. Unfortunately, transparency does not necessarily mean accuracy. When everything can be measured, it will sometimes be more difficult to make sense out of the measures. It will also be easier to manipulate them to support your own point of view.

Citizens will be able to monitor their own bodies and the air quality around them, for example, as well as many other variables they think are important. The underlying architecture of pervasive computing networks has no center, grows from the edges, and cannot be controlled. When the tools of measurement become pervasive, almost anything will be measured. It will be difficult to tell, however, when the transparency will be truthful and when it will be self-promoting (or both). Pervasive computing will provide the tools for transparency, but others will shape how those measurement tools get used— including regulators, advocacy groups, and those being measured.

Michael Conroy has explored this territory in great depth in his book *Branded!*[3] Non-governmental organizations (commonly called NGOs) are creating new ways of monitoring and evaluating corporations. Global corporate branding and the global reach of brands make it impossible for single countries to regulate. NGOs are introducing their own certification systems: Fair Trade Certified monitors coffee and chocolate; Marine Stewardship Council encourages sustainable fishing practices; Health Care Without Harm and the Green Guide for Health Care promote environmentally friendly health care. This certification revolution will apply pervasive computing tools to reshape the kind of transparency that is possible. And what a given NGO looks for when measuring will be based on the values that they are advocating—which could narrow or broaden the public agenda.

Corporations and their leaders will be under much more scrutiny in this world. But there will also be new opportunities to work across companies, perhaps across industries, to establish new commons for trading that fit within the constraints of certification. Industry associations, for example, will have new opportunities to use pervasive computing to provide shared measures around important topics like safety. While corporations and NGOs will always be adversaries to some extent, it will also be possible to establish shared assets that benefit all concerned.

The big wave of change is toward open rather than closed. Not everything will be completely open, however. Open source thinking will be a fundamental driver of change in the future and it will add to and complicate the move toward transparency. Quiet transparency implies a significant degree of openness. It is based on a premise of trust that, if you give ideas away, you will get even better ideas back in return. Open source logic teaches that leaders will need to release exclusive ownership and have the faith to be transparent. In addition, they must contribute to a greater good which is emerging but not yet apparent. Leaders need to be able to use open source thinking to raise the bar for competition.

Combine open source thinking with pervasive computing—a world with wireless connectivity and sensors everywhere—and you get many new opportunities to interact, exchange, and collaborate. New possibilities will emerge as market demand and fear come together. For example, concerns about global climate change will result in the need to monitor progress or decline in a way that is trustworthy. New groups will arise to take on this responsibility. Will they be able to work together? That is the dilemma, but the potential is very encouraging.

ECOSYSTEMS TRANSPARENCY

In the future, every environmental characteristic that can be measured will be measured—by somebody. There is the potential for much more data with a greater level of detail. Imagine that every house as you walk down the street, for example, had an indicator on the outside showing how much energy that household is using on a yearly, monthly, daily, or even minute-by-minute basis. The questions with such a system will be: who is doing the measuring? Will it be voluntary? Will everyone use the same standards? Will transparency for ecosystems be quiet or self-promoting or both?

Large-scale environmental sensing projects are already under-
way. For example, the National Ecological Observatory Network
(NEON) is laying the groundwork for distributing monitors of ecological systems continent-wide. MIT's Media Lab is pursuing what
they call "wikicity" projects that combine data feeds from local utili-
ties and services to show how much energy is used in major metropolitan areas. Australia's Commonwealth Scientific and Industrial
Research Organisation (CSIRO) has a Catchment Modeling Toolkit,
which provides open source modules for modeling water consumption. These are just a few examples from IFTF's current Ten-Year
Forecast, but we expect many more over the next decade. The tools
of transparency will be everywhere.

Personal cell phones, for example, will be equipped with sensors
to gather data in the field. Intel Research is doing an experiment right
now with cell phone sensing devices to monitor pollution down to
the level of a city block, a particular building, and potentially even
individual rooms. The vast mobile network of cell phone users could
be repurposed for pollution monitoring, with much more specific
focus. Now, pollution levels tend to be measured by central sensors
at the level of a city or region by corporate, government, or news
organizations. In the near future, anyone could measure air quality
and distribute the results—which may not be pleasant for those being
measured. With sensors everywhere, environmental activists, community organizations, or health care agencies could organize citizen
sensor networks around a variety of concerns.

You would be able to evaluate external air quality and track the
amount of pollutants that your body can handle. Jason Tester at IFTF
created an artifact from the future that models a handheld device that
could advise an individual user "You should go inside within ten minutes" when pollution levels get too high for that particular person.
Such services could be offered and supported by local health care
providers or even local community or religious groups. Our forecasts
suggest that there will be an increasing number of "biocitizens," consumers whose concerns blend both personal health and environmental sustainability. Many will take it upon themselves to be watchdogs,

using inexpensive sensors to measure what they think is important or dangerous.

A major challenge with all of this new data from ecological monitoring systems is how we will analyze and interpret the massive amount of data. Transparency suggests that we will see through the actions of leaders and organizations. Pervasive computing will help us measure what we are seeing. But who will help us make sense out of what we have seen? Certainly, a large array of governmental, advocacy, and corporate groups will have points of view on what the data is saying. Companies, however, will have limited control over what gets measured and how the results are perceived.

Leaders Who Demonstrate Quiet Transparency

Leaders who are quietly transparent are hard to discover because they don't advertise themselves. I realize this is a dilemma: leaders need to be known in order to lead; yet they should not be self-promotional. A strong resume is wonderful for a leader, but it is much more powerful if someone else discovers it. In fact, the most productive and happiest leaders may be those who are "undiscovered." Quiet leaders do not face the pressures of their more publicity-oriented counterparts. They are content to lead quietly while others get the attention. The drawback to a lack of recognition is that they may not be having as much impact as they could. The core dilemma is this: how do you reach your full leadership potential without advertising yourself?

One leader who demonstrates quiet transparency is Ellen Galinsky, president and cocreator of the Families and Work Institute (FWI), a nonprofit in New York City. Ellen has explored the space between work and private life. She reframed this work/life "balance" as work/life "navigation," since balance is really impossible to achieve. The interactions between work and private life are not a problem that can be solved, but rather an ongoing ever-changing dilemma that must be managed. Navigation implies that there are some fixed obstacles that must be avoided, but that there are also currents that are fluid and lots of choices regarding what to do. Work/life navigation is a clear and useful term, since it frames the life choices of a career very clearly, but gives lots of room for individual variation. Navigation involves both fixed hazards and fluid currents, with lots of options for personal choice.

Ellen Galinsky is very energetic and outgoing, but she is not self-promoting. She writes, speaks, and organizes to spread her message. FWI has contributed to the human resource strategies of many major organizations and is transparent in the sense that it shares all of its research. Both Ellen and FWI have a quietly transparent style. They are engaged and open, but they don't oversell themselves.

I met Ellen on a panel at a conference on the implications of working from home. The next morning, I saw her on the *Today Show* talking about a new government policy for those who work at home. Ellen is one of the key people to be interviewed whenever issues arise around work and private life. People come to her. She is a person of renown, but she is also a humble public figure who doesn't take herself too seriously. Her style is understated by design. Her career is an example of how one can become an authority on a single substantive issue without developing an inflated ego.[4]

Timberland is a corporation that demonstrates transparency in its own low-key way. They don't hype their greenness, but anyone who is interested can see that they are environmentally responsible. Their mission statement gives a clear sense of their orientation and style, which is understated:

> Our mission is to equip people to make a difference in their world. . . . Our place in this world is bigger than the things we put in it . . . Making new products goes hand in hand with making things better. That means reducing our carbon footprint and being as environmentally responsible as we can. We love every minute we spend outdoors, and we work hard to create things that make that experience better in every way.[5]

The people of Timberland like hiking, which is why they make boots. They also like the outdoors, which is why they were one of the first to calculate their own carbon footprint. Timberland is a large

OUR FOOTPRINT *NOTRE EMPREINTE*

Climate Impact[1] *Incidences sur le climat[1]*

Use of renewable energy	
Utilisation d'énergie renouvelable	6.36%

Chemicals Used[2] *Produits chimiques utilisés[2]*

PVC-free *Sans PVC*	81.14%

Resource Consumption *Consommation de ressources*

Eco-conscious materials[3]	
Matériaux écologiques[3]	5.27%
Recycled content of shoebox	
Contenu en matières recyclées de la boîte de chaussures	100%

Trees planted through 2007
***Nombre d'arbres plantés en 2007*   668,225**

For more information visit www.timberland.com/footprint
Pour plus d'information : www.timberland.com/footprint

[1] *Measured against approximately 14% of Timberland's total climate impact for 2008. (excludes, e.g., licensees and third party factories).*
Mesuré contre 14% environ de l'impact de climat total de Timberland pour le compte de l'année 2008. (À l'exclusion, par exemple, des détenteurs de permis et des usines de tierces parties)

[2] *Footwear skus produced in 2007. Measure excludes trace elements.*
Modèles de chaussures fabriqués en 2007. La mesure exclut les oligo-éléments.

[3] *Footwear skus produced in 2007 with at least 10% recycled, renewable and/or organic materials in one or more components. Look for the eco-conscious icons.*
Modèles de chaussures fabriqués en 2007 contenant au moins 10% de matériau recyclé, renouvelable ou organique, dans une ou plusieurs parties de la chaussure. Recherchez les symboles écologiques.

Timberland footwear includes: Timberland and non-licensed Timberland PRO.
Les chaussures Timberland comprennent : Timberland et Timberland PRO.

Printed on 100% post consumer recycled material.
Imprimé sur matériau recyclé post-consommation à 100%.

FIGURE 16. Timberland's measurement of the company's carbon footprint. *Source:* Used with permission of Timberland.

company with a quietly transparent style. When you walk in the woods, you walk quietly if you want to see the wildlife all around you. If you advertise your environmental values too loudly, you will become a target for critics. The Timberland carbon footprint label has become a model for transparency.

Quiet Transparency Summary

There is one big lesson from quiet transparency: if leaders advertise themselves and take credit for their own performances, they will become targets. British Petroleum learned this when the company changed its name to BP, for "Beyond Petroleum." BP did a lot to live up to its new name, with many creative efforts around sustainability. Taking that bold position with regard to environmental policies, however, did little to advance relations with advocacy groups or regulators. In fact, this self-promotion seemed to make people even harder on BP, which was sometimes perceived as a soft target.

This example teaches us this: do the right thing and be transparent, but don't be self-promotional. Be willing to tell others what you are doing and why, but only when they ask. Anyone who is interested is more likely to see what you are doing and believe what you say. As a leader, you will need to make it easy for third-party organizations to notice your transparency as well as spread the word to others.

There are no sure things, but quiet transparency makes it more likely that leaders will succeed. We will still have leaders who act like rock stars and they may gain fame, but they will also become big targets and are much more likely to come and go quickly. Those who try to advertise their own good works are putting themselves and their organizations at risk. Humble strength is a much better leadership quality for the future.

Leaders will make the future, in their own quiet ways. Sometimes, they will not get credit for the futures they make. The world of the future will not always be fair—but it never has been. Leaders with self-promotional transparency may get more attention for brief periods, but I doubt they will be more successful in the long run. Quiet transparency will be the best way to lead.

8

Rapid Prototyping

Ability to create quick early versions of innovations,
with the expectation that later success will require early failures.

WHEN I TOOK MY FIRST computer programming class in 1970 at Northwestern, the professor noted that the two best programmers he had ever seen had extremely different strategies. One would carefully write out and mentally test his program before submitting it (these were the days of batch process where you brought your card deck to a large central computer). The other would do a quick and dirty version and submit it right away, to get the diagnosis of what did not work. The latter approach was rapid prototyping.

Rapid prototyping enables us to learn from failure quickly, again and again. It is the trial-and-error method that has always been important for innovators, but on a faster cycle. The motto of rapid prototyping is fail early, fail often, and fail cheaply.

Rapid prototyping is a perfect leadership style for the VUCA world—where truth emerges from engagement, trial, and error—because it allows leaders to try out their own ideas quickly, as well as tap into the maker instincts of potential collaborators.

Few leaders get it right the first time, and it will get even harder in the future. Early failure is often key to later success. The failures of "computer conferencing" in the 1970s contributed to the eventual success of MySpace and Facebook, for example. This lesson from failure took a very long time, however. In the future, leaders need to speed up the process. They should expect to go through multiple iterations of everything. As Alan Kay was known for saying when he was at Xerox PARC, "the purpose of research is to fail, but to fail in an interesting way." Rapid prototyping is all about failing in interesting ways.

Rapid Prototyping Defined

Rapid prototyping is a quick cycle of innovation and refinement. Rapid prototypes typically have lifetimes measured in hours or days, not months. They are different from pilot or demonstration projects, which often take much longer to conduct.

Rapid prototyping is the maker instinct applied to innovation. While the concept of do-it-yourself is still important, the next generation of innovation will be driven by "do-it-ourselves" leaders who don't get stuck on idea ownership since in this process people's ideas get mixed quickly and it is often impossible to sort out who thought of what.

Leaders can learn from people's pains, and innovation can help to relieve those pains. In rapid prototyping, the emphasis is not on abstract thought about possibilities or plans; it should begin with real people, with the end users out in the field, and as early as possible in the process. It is more about listening than it is about thinking.

Companies can learn a lot from watching and listening to what people do with their products. Users are a remarkable source of new ideas for improving upon and reinventing products and services. The people who actually use a product can be a source of insight if companies are willing to learn along with them. The corporate instinct is often to control one's products, but that is an instinct that should be resisted. Manufacturers make the products, but no longer own them once they are purchased. The new owners may change them or use them in new ways. The innovation cycle is not necessarily over when the product is sold. Leadership through rapid prototyping

- Is characterized by a trial-and-error mentality with an interest in getting something started quickly. Leaders expect to fail early in the process so they can succeed later;
- Emphasizes experience in the field, rather than massive advance planning;
- Maximizes education by putting priority on extreme speed in learning.

Traditional leadership has always put a premium on thinking things through before acting. In military battles, as I understand it, the rule of thumb is typically "one third, two thirds," where one third of the time is spent planning a mission, and the other two thirds is used for preparation in the field. It is tempting, even in battle, to spend more time planning and less time preparing. Rapid prototyping goes the other way: leaders should minimize planning, but maximize preparing in low-risk settings and learning in the field. The rule of thumb for rapid prototyping is less planning, more learn-as-you-go action.

At IFTF, our former president Roy Amara often employed what he called the "jump to the end" strategy with a new project. As we began a six-month project, for example, Roy would say something like: "Let's do the entire project in a day. Then, we'll come back and fill in the holes and decide what to do next." It was an outrageous suggestion: do a six-month project in a day. But when we tried, we learned things about the project that we never could have imagined until we dove in. Rapid prototyping is learning by doing, but it is also doing by learning. It is a messy process, but it is also invigorating.

Often the best way to do rapid prototyping is through the use of simulation or gaming, utilizing realistic but low-risk learning environments. Rapid prototyping fits very well with the future leadership skill called immersive learning ability, which was described in chapter 4. Leaders with immersive learning ability will find it much easier to do rapid prototyping. When faced with a new challenge, they could think of it as a game and immerse themselves in it. When I used to play basketball, we prepared for the next week's game by creating a "scout team" in practice. The scout team's job would be to simulate our opponents and run their plays. Scout team members would model their play on specific players from the other team. Our team would scrimmage against the scout team as a way of preparing our strategies and tactics of attack for the game—true rapid prototyping in action. Great practice teams usually do well during games because they have already prototyped and practiced in a realistic situation. Teams that spend too much time in the locker room planning and not enough time out on the court are at a disadvantage. The real learning happens on the court.

Dilemmas in the Future

Rapid prototyping is an essential methodology for making the future. When I began my career in the early 1970s, much of the leading-edge innovation conducted at universities was funded by ARPA (Advanced Research Projects Agency, the research army of the Department of Defense). Innovation was top-down, driven and guided by central government policy. Leadership was centralized and hierarchical. Now, just forty or so years later, it's become much more decentralized. Innovation tends to happen bottom-up, fueled by consumer electronics, gaming, and the maker instincts of many.

Leaders have to learn how to try and fail, then try again—all with a smile, or at least an expectation of much iteration. Of course, simulations and immersive environments can help leaders try and fail in low-risk ways, but try and fail we must—in order to ultimately succeed.

PROTOTYPING IN DIASPORAS

Rapid prototyping works well within a diaspora because ideas spread more rapidly across a community of shared values and trusted relationships. News of the performance of a new beauty product, for example, will spread much more quickly among family members who find the product beneficial. Testing a new idea is easier with a diaspora because it will circulate at a faster rate and reach a greater number of people. Diasporas are innovation breeding grounds if the innovations are a good fit with their values, priorities, financial resources, and availability of time.

Within a diaspora, rapid prototyping can begin with a small number of people but swiftly spread to many more. A diaspora could be considered an army of potential prototypers. Active diasporas will make aggressive use of networked media. Offshore Chinese or Indian people, for example, are separated geographically from their homeland, but once they are joined electronically, word spreads in a flash.

FINANCIAL PROTOTYPING CAN BE DANGEROUS

Innovation in the world of finance can be very dangerous. The mortgage crisis of 2008, for example, was fueled by financial innovation gone amok. Mortgages were intended as long-term financial agreements between a home buyer and a bank or other institution giving the loan. As financial "innovation" accelerated, however, these long-term instruments were packaged and sold to others, creating a growing chain of debt instruments that could be traded on a short-term basis. When the system started to break down, it was hard to know where to turn, since the original long-term instruments had been packaged and repackaged for market trading that certainly benefitted some people along the way until things fell apart. People were encouraged to buy homes they could not afford in order to fuel the market for a kind of trading that looked a lot like gambling. These complex mortgage instruments were certainly creative and innovative, but they also created awful dilemmas down the road.

In public settings, it is tempting to borrow ahead rather than pay taxes today—even though the costs to future generations will be high. The current taboo on tax increases makes it more likely that financial "innovation" will grow to help improve infrastructure without increasing taxes. The danger is that the innovation will hide new risk, just as it did with the mortgage crisis.

Rapid prototyping could help financial institutions, but caution is appropriate because the risks are so high. Often, prototyping in the world of finance happens in the market, where the definition of what works is who makes money.

PROTOTYPING IN CIVIC SOCIETY

In the United States, compelling anecdotes drive policy-making. When a bridge collapses, there is a great public outcry and an immediate discussion of who is to blame and what can be done to prevent further collapses in the future. Unfortunately, however, it is very difficult to sustain the sense of urgency long enough to pass legislation to support the rebuilding and upkeep for infrastructure—until the next disaster happens. When demands increase but taxes don't, something else must be done to finance new infrastructure, and that something is not likely to play out well in the long run. The idea of rapid prototyping will often work better in business than in public policy.

Pilot and demonstration projects are often very useful to explore new policy ideas; rapid prototyping, however, moves much more quickly. New policies will be worked out in the field and rapid prototyping will be an important way to test out new ideas.

The first year of the Maker Faire was a different kind of public space prototype. The organizers tried a variety of approaches, all in the context of the Faire. The concepts evolved as the event scaled up to 70,000 participants and now is being expanded to include other cities. At the first Maker Faire, it was not at all obvious what the event would become. Rapid prototyping provided a way to try out new concepts in low-risk ways, with a trust that what emerged would be interesting in ways that had not been anticipated.

OPEN SOURCE WARFARE

Terrorist groups really get the concept of rapid prototyping. Insurgent warfare is focused on surprise and soft targets. Insurgent warriors try lots of tactics, and if one works, the new tactic spreads rapidly. If the terrorist group is a diaspora, the prototype results circulate even faster.

In the world of open source asymmetrical warfare, the tactics will come from everywhere. Weapons will not just be traditional military-designed tools of war. Consumer electronics, games, and cell phones are the current weapons platforms of choice for many insurgent groups. In future warfare, rapid prototyping will be common terrorist strategy—which means that citizens and peacekeeping forces will need readiness training to prepare for surprise from many different directions.

Branches of the U.S. military and many other public service agencies, including police and fire departments, use a formal method called "After Action Reviews" (AARs) as a discipline for learning from everyday experiences.[1] AARs fit very well with rapid prototyping, since they focus on learning from failures. Unlike performance reviews, AARs are focused only on what can be learned and what can be improved. AARs explicitly avoid the subject of blame. The army does keep a central database of lessons from AARs over the years, but the real value of AARs is not the database but the discipline.

As best I can tell, many army personnel participate in several AARs every day, one for every significant experience, it seems; or there is at least informal learning that takes place. AARs can be used very effectively as the feedback loop in the rapid prototyping process. Indeed, this discipline fits in well with learning from the early failures and applying those lessons to achieve later success. In the world of warfare, AARs mean that the lessons from insurgent attacks can be quickly learned and reapplied in the field.

AAR discipline works well in the military, police, and fire services, but I've never seen a private corporation practice it efficiently. Why? Most corporations are not able to separate learning from evaluation. They may have policies stating that it is important to learn from failures, but in reality employees know that if they fall short they will be punished. Failure is accepted in theory, but in practice it is almost universally unrecognized. The only exceptions I've seen are Silicon Valley companies, where failure is often seen as a badge of courage. If you haven't failed in Silicon Valley, it means you haven't taken enough risks, but the AAR approach would be too structured for them.

ORGANIZATIONS DESIGNED FOR PROTOTYPING

Some organizations within large corporations are now designed to do rapid prototyping. P&G FutureWorks, for example, is a central group focused on potential new products and service innovations that P&G might consider beyond its current categories. The leader of this group, Nathan Estruth, comes from a background in political science and political campaigns. By nature, Nathan is an organizer with a keen interest in new ideas, working in the context of a very large corporation.

Rapid prototyping is basic to FutureWorks. I remember in the early days of their work, they were deciding whether or not to go into the energy bar market. At that point, they wanted to learn as much as they could about energy bars. The idea was to try out lots of options, and they fully expected to fail "early, often, and cheaply," as was the motto in those days. They set up a room in their very flexible space that was dedicated to energy bars. Since I use them myself when I travel, I was very interested. When I went into the room, I saw more energy bars than I knew were in existence. Everyone one on the FutureWorks team was using energy bars as part of their lifestyle, just to try out the concept. In parallel, they created a series of prototype energy bars that they tried out themselves, while also testing them with a variety of their target end users. The first step in rapid prototyping is immersion in the world of end users with the aim of understanding their priorities, their pain, and their hopes. The second step is to begin prototyping to use the collected data to check assumptions made earlier. P&G decided not to pursue energy bars because it was impossible to isolate the benefits of the bar from the behavior of the person. The best of the bars worked, but only if the consumer developed an exercise program as well. Getting people to exercise is a lot harder than getting them to eat a tasty healthy bar.

Rapid prototyping should begin and stay as close as possible to the end consumers. For example (and it is an extreme example), when Nathan Estruth and his team created a new gravy dog food for the Iams brand, they literally ate dog food themselves as they developed the prototypes—as well as feeding the new food to dogs.

Rapid prototyping requires leaders to amplify their teams as much as possible—to immerse themselves in the future worlds they are trying to create. For example, Humana has created a large innovation space where they gather all the possible health enhancement products and services that they have discovered around the world. This is a much larger space than the FutureWorks room for energy bars; the Humana space is laid out so that staff can actually try out all the devices, games, and products. It is a kind of petting zoo for future health aids. It is a simulator that can be configured to test new concepts.

For example, when I was there they were working with the Wii Fit program and a number of similar systems, which they tested in senior citizen centers, working with both seniors and kids. This is an interesting time in the gaming industry—the Wii is fueling a shift from serious gamers to casual users to a range of people like these seniors who are not gamers at all. The prototypes Humana is testing use engaging software to encourage movement in a playful and stimulating way, as prompted by the system and the social setting. The best way to learn about these potential innovations is to try them out among the potential end users.

VISUAL PROTOTYPING

Rapid prototyping will benefit greatly from the tremendous improvements in our tools for visualization that will happen over the next decade. Visualization is a form of rapid prototyping in your mind and in virtual space. Pioneering work in this field is being done by The Grove Consultants International, founded by organization consultant and information designer David Sibbet.[2] This organization teaches people to use visualization to imagine future possibilities and bring them to life in what could be called visual cartography. The Grove provides leaders with a method to rapidly prototype their own thinking and evolve their own organizational stories about how things work in their world—similar to the way a design firm would prototype a new product. Conceptual prototyping can be just as effective as product prototyping, for many of the same reasons. Along the way,

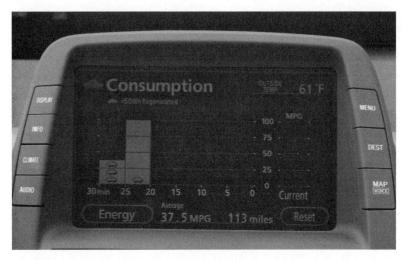

FIGURE 17. Dashboard of a Toyota Prius showing gasoline consumption.
Source: Used with permission of Toyota.

The Grove has developed graphic templates that help people imagine new strategies and make them practical.

Stimulated by new visual tools, leaders will be able to improve their visual literacy—the ability to understand and communicate in pictures, drawings, and other forms of imagery. Visualization, like other pervasive computing tools, will be available in much more decentralized ways and at far less cost. The new visual tools will allow much more realistic forms of rapid prototyping in virtual and enhanced worlds. Visual computing will also allow many things to be visible that were invisible before.

An example is the dashboard of the Toyota Prius, which shows a real-time display of gasoline consumption while you drive. Behavior change happens best when it is influenced by immediate feedback, which is exactly what the Prius dashboard gives to a driver. In fact, it is sometimes difficult to concentrate while driving a Prius because it is so tempting to look over at the display and try to influence it with your driving. My guess is that that dashboard has saved a lot of fuel, but a few accidents have been caused because the display is so engaging to watch.

Imagine a Prius-like dashboard that visualizes the measures that are most important for the organization you lead. You could use this tool to test changes that you might make as a leader. In a virtual visual world, you could reap the benefits of rapid prototyping without the risk of actually making those changes out in the real world. Of course, there is the challenge of designing virtual worlds that accurately reflect the real world.

A Rapid Prototyping Leader

Institute for the Future is located just a block from IDEO—arguably the world's leading design firm—in downtown Palo Alto, California. IDEO is a model for rapid prototyping. "IDEO University" teaches rapid prototyping as a way of engaging people in the design and innovation process.

IDEO's workspace is unique. Founder David Kelley believes that design groups should be no bigger than about thirty people and that each studio should be designed in a way that adds to the creativity of the group. One design group used their office furnishings budget to purchase the tailpiece from an old DC-3 aircraft. Another purchased heavy curtains from a theater that was going out of business. My favorite studio at IDEO is a gutted Volkswagen bus rebuilt as a work environment, created as a joke on a designer while he was on vacation. This combination of good design and playfulness is stimulating and very helpful for rapid prototyping.

Rapid prototyping shows up in all the products that IDEO has designed. About a hundred versions of the Palm Pilot are on display at the Palo Alto office, from a crude foam cutout to a machine shop prototype to a commercial product. Seeing all of them together, one gets a sense of the evolution from first idea to final product. The failures along the way reveal lessons that get built into the next generation of the prototype.

IFTF has worked together with IDEO on several different projects. Thinking ten years ahead, we provide the foresight, which IDEO incorporates into their prototyping process. Essentially, we are looking for waves of social change that can be ridden by the product.

Rapid prototyping typically begins with ethnographic study of real people in their native habitat—the environment in which the product will be used.

One project we worked on involved the creation of healthy, portable, and inexpensive food. First IDEO looked at current products. Cheerios with nonfat milk scored pretty well on the nutrition and price scales, for example—but they are not very portable. IDEO then combined consumer insight with foresight to help generate new ideas. From the first day of the project, they were roughing out prototypes, using any material that could be easily formed and reformed. Each studio has a "tech box" that contains materials that their designers have collected from all over the world to use in creating new prototypes.

IDEO has institutionalized rapid prototyping, though their designers have avoided over-standardizing it. This learn-as-you-go spirit lets the process of creativity happen without trying to control it.

Rapid Prototyping Summary

Rapid prototyping is a practical way to tap into the maker instinct to organize an ongoing process of innovation. Leaders with maker instinct will get the idea of rapid prototyping easily and use it to succeed. The big challenge will be for them to accept failures as important ingredients to success and learn from them. Many leaders do not like failure of any kind, but in the future, they will have to change their expectations and learn to play through them.

Leadership in the future will be about high-speed, perpetual prototyping. The best leaders will be those who embrace the process and develop the ability to discern the patterns across the prototypes, the ideas that really do work. As Winston Churchill said, "Success is the ability to go from failure to failure with no loss of enthusiasm."[4]

9

Smart Mob Organizing

Ability to create, engage with, and nurture
purposeful business or social change networks
through intelligent use of electronic and other media.

WHEN I WAS IN GRADUATE SCHOOL, Saul Alinsky was an iconic community organizer working on the south side of Chicago. He was the model for social activism. We have not yet seen the Saul Alinsky of cyberspace. It may be that his counterpart in cyberspace turns out to be a network, rather than a single person. Tomorrow's version of community organizing will be smart mob organizing. We are beginning to see this today, but the smart mobs of the future will much smarter.

Leaders are what they can organize. They make connections and draw links. Everyone is part of a network and electronic media will amplify networks for business or social change. Future leaders will be expert users of the next generation of online social media that will be foreign to many current leaders.

Some social networks will have intense values linkages, so leadership must mesh with those values, some of which will be competing. Indeed, leaders' own networks and connections will be their most powerful assets. This has always been true to some extent, but the connections in the future will be amplified.

Smart mob organizing starts with choosing the medium that is appropriate to the situation. Most of today's leaders communicate well in person, but have a range of skills using electronic media. Leaders of the future must have a strong online identity, as well as a compelling in-person presence. Younger people are more likely to have strong online identities, since they grew up with the web. The electronic media are not, by themselves, what makes a smart mob smart. The leaders and participants in the smart mob provide the intelligence, but the media amplify that intelligence. Powerful collaboration technologies are now practical, after more than thirty years of testing. Smart mob organizing is the maker instinct applied to social connectivity and network making. Solo makers are coming together into smart mobs of makers. All that maker energy has the potential to be channeled in new and highly creative ways, if leaders are able to figure out how to tap into it.

Smart Mob Organizing Defined

Smart mob organizing brings together large groups for a common business or social change purpose, making savvy use of available media as appropriate. They are smart because the media amplify their collective intelligence for greater impact. They are mobs because their behavior is emergent and often unpredictable. Of course, smart mobs can be more or less intelligent—depending on the resources of the members, the talent of the leaders, and the effectiveness of their media.

The father of this concept is Bay Area visionary Howard Rheingold, who in 2003 coined the term in his very important book, *Smart Mobs.*[1] With remarkable speed, "smart mobs" entered the vocabulary to the point where I saw it used in major publications within one year of the book's release, without quotation marks and without attribution.

Howard Rheingold's web site (www.smartmobs.com) continues to explore the evolution of smart mobs. Rheingold calls them "the power of the mobile many." Now, barely five years after it was introduced, some experts in the field say that the term has become dated. I disagree. It can be transformative when a leadership team, an NGO, or an industry association reimagines itself as a smart mob. Terms like "smart mobs" are also provocative; they get people to think about the future and to realize that not all mobs are smart, nor are they necessarily well-intentioned. Unfortunately, hostile mobs often seem more sophisticated in their use of new media than do positive smart mobs.

As forecasters, we seek out terms that provoke people constructively without turning them off. Referring to "smart networks" or "smart connectivity" would tap into the same space, but would not be as provocative as "smart mobs." Merely using those words can start a very interesting conversation about leadership in the future.

Face-to-face meetings are still useful at some stages in smart mob organizing, especially for orientation and trust building, but often they are not possible. Luckily, the range of media options is getting much wider and the new media work much better than they used to. Organizing smart mobs is already practical, and it will become required for effective leadership in the future. Consider the following example from today, but presaging tomorrow.

Lyn Jeffery, the cultural anthropologist at IFTF I mentioned earlier, is studying the Chinese language Internet. One of the disruptions that she observed is the growing popularity of "tuangous," which are smart mobs organized to buy things. One of the earliest cases was a group of about thirty people who all wanted to buy new BMWs. The tuangou went to a BMW dealer and asked "What is the price if we buy thirty all at once?" This was not a pleasant question for the BMW dealer, since it was not the model of retail that he had in mind.

Tuangous are now starting to organize to purchase much less expensive products and services. They come together, often through the Internet, around a particular purchasing need. Leadership emerges on an ad hoc basis, and there is clear benefit for all of the buyers. This kind of smart mob is changing the rules of the marketplace.

Dilemmas in the Future

Smart mobs and not-so-smart mobs will become much more common over the next decade. Leaders will need to learn the skills of smart mob organizing and develop their own online presence and leadership styles. In-person leadership will not be enough.

SMART MOBS IN CIVIL SOCIETY

Howard Dean's early campaign in 2004 was groundbreaking in its use of the Internet, and it established models that spread quickly. The 2008 election, however, was the first to make heavy use of media for smart mob organizing; the techniques were more creative and the platforms more stable. This, however, was just the beginning of smart mob politics in civil society. Expect much more in future elections.

Barack Obama's 2008 campaign proved the value of online smart mobs for fund-raising, making very sophisticated use of social media to organize for their candidate. Neither Obama nor his opponent, John McCain, was a natural in these media, and neither grew up with them. Obama, however, invested much more time and effort, and his followers skewed young, which helped accelerate the campaign's use of the Internet.

At one time, YouTube was mostly "gotcha" videos that caught candidates or endorsers saying the wrong thing at the wrong time. In the 2008 presidential campaign, we all learned about the downside risk of a candidate receiving endorsements from anyone who had ever said something stupid on video. By this criterion, it will be difficult to get any endorsements at all in the future, and it will be increasingly difficult to find anyone who has *not* said something stupid on video.

Smart mobs can amplify misinformation just as rapidly as they can spread the truth. The take-home lesson: smart mobs can boost a candidate rapidly, but other smart mobs can bring that same leader down just as fast. Smart mobs are not necessarily fair, nor are they necessarily right. Sometimes, they will be dumb—depending on your point of view.

The new civil society will have platforms that allow much greater participation across the population, for better or for worse. The founders of the United States were skeptical about direct democracy—saying it was just not possible—which is why they created a system based on representatives. The founders were very leery about mobs. Pervasive social media, however, create new potential for direct democracy. Smart mobs (or dumb mobs) could soon become the carriers of the people's message. Electronic media will soon make direct democracy possible and perhaps even practical. The new media may, in effect, challenge the founders' logic and give us a structure that allows full participation. Do we really want a more direct democracy? Smart mobs are already forming and creating new modes of civil engagement. Using rapid prototyping to create a new form of civil media-enhanced society, smart mobs will have their say—like it or not.

I doubt that the United States will adopt a governmental structure run by smart mobs—even if it does become possible. Still, that will be the direction of change over the next ten years. The good news is that the new networks make it possible to collaborate and cooperate in ways that were never before available. The bad news is that destructive mobs will be active as well, and they tend to have highly developed media skills.

A SMART MOB FOR HEALTH

Most households are very concerned about health, and the person most often at the center of the household is, according to most research, Mom (whether or not she is literally a mother). Indeed, some of the groups we work with that develop new health products now refer to the "HMM," or "Health Management Mom" (a play on the old Health Management Organization, or HMO). The mom-led health smart mob for a particular family includes not only the family physician, but also specialists (when they are needed), family, friends, retailers who give advice, online medical sources, and online communities. Our forecasts suggest that health insecurity will grow in all parts of the world, which will create more need for health-oriented smart mobs.

The challenge on a larger scale is to create a health-and-wellness platform that allows smart mobs to form, re-form, and multiply. At this time in the United States, the closest thing we have to this is the Centers for Disease Control and Prevention (the CDC), which is indeed focusing on creating a new culture of health—as well as responding to disease threats. There are also a number of virtual smart mobs for health arising—most of them targeting people suffering from particular medical conditions. Web sites like www.mydaughtersdna.org and www.patientslikeme.com are efforts to organize smart mobs to manage sickness. Indeed, sharing information with others who have similar health issues has been, still is, and will continue to be a very important use for the Internet.

Kelly Traver is a physician focused on health and wellness who could not find a way to sustain a wellness-oriented practice within the traditional financial structure of the health care system in the United States—which is actually more of a sick care system.[2]

Dr. Traver organized a kind of smart mob around healthy living. She created her own start-up as the first prototype of a new kind of health commons, currently called MD Health Evolution, where the principles of healthy living can become a shared asset for much larger groups of people. She began by providing health coaching to Google's employees. Now she is working with a range of companies and broadening her approach to spreading the twelve principles of healthy living that she has developed.

I participated in the prototype for MD Health Evolution and was very impressed. I already had some pretty good healthy living practices, but her twelve principles are the best summary I have ever seen. More importantly, the principles are packaged with a process and delivered in a practical way that I found easy to apply. The principles provide the content, but a smart mob of healthy living practitioners will be necessary to spread the word and the behaviors.

I don't believe that there is any single path to health and fitness, but I found this program both solid and flexible enough to help me change a number of my behaviors in a more healthy direction. In effect, I've formed my own little smart mob (with coaching from a handful of others) that is focused on my health. I am also part of a smart mob that Dr. Traver is organizing to make sure these principles reach a much larger portion of society.

Over the next ten years, a global health economy will emerge as a major economic driver. Within this economy, smart mobs will organize and spread health practices in unusual ways that are likely to have major social benefits.

ON THE SIDE OF OPENNESS

The term "open source" comes from open source software, which refers to source code under a license that permits others to study, change, and improve the software—under the condition that they share improvements with the creator and others. Open source as a principle is not an either/or choice; it is a sliding scale from completely open to completed closed. Leaders will decide where they want to fit on that scale. The forecast map inside the book jacket reflects the future force of openness. Smart mobs will accelerate the trend toward increasing openness. You cannot control a mob.

Open source practices still need to have a structure of some kind. For example, in the world of R&D, a very interesting range of open source networks has emerged, such as InnoCentive. InnoCentive is a kind of highly structured smart mob of scientists interested in ad hoc assignments for pay. They are prequalified for participation in an open source network of scientific problem solvers. Companies offer bounties for solutions to chemistry problems, or other specific tasks. Scientists in the network bid on the work and InnoCentive manages the transactions.

YourEncore is similar, but uses only retired scientists from R&D organizations in top companies. YourEncore is particularly fascinating, since it also provides meaningful work opportunities for scientists who are officially retired but still want to work in the field of science, although under new terms of engagement. Thus, it is a bridge between individual scientists and corporations with specific R&D needs. YourEncore makes it easier to form smart mobs that match retired scientists with tasks they could do for hire. It represents individual scientists looking for meaningful work, as well as the corporations looking for support in their scientific endeavors. YourEncore also feeds the corporate and scientific diasporas of which the individual scientists are a part.

These open source efforts are highly structured and focused, yet they are also smart mobs with the purpose of delivering high quality ad hoc R&D services in a decentralized pay-for-the-task structure. One could argue that these mobs are very smart since they are mostly scientists with graduate degrees.

SMART MOBS AT WAR

Terrorist groups can be smart mobs too. In fact, from a purely sociological point of view, many of the terrorist groups are very sophisticated indeed in their use of new media, in spite of some of the religious beliefs that call for return to a simpler time. Many of these smart, but threatening, mobs are far ahead of more moderate groups. Network-based warfare is now a mainstream practice, and there are few rules of engagement that can be trusted. It is currently more explicit, however, than the forms of war that are likely to emerge over the next decade.

Meme warfare, for example, is likely to be carried by smart mobs. Memes are self-propagating ideas that spread like a virus. Vannevar Bush wrote a classic article right after World War II envisioning the "Memex" to allow ideas to be shared across large communities.[3] In this groundbreaking article Bush imagined a network like the Internet long before 1968 when its precursor began. Richard Dawkins used the term in 1976, drawing from the fundamentals of natural selection. Meme warfare will add a nasty twist to mob organizing:

> The point of conventional warfare is, in the words of George Patton, "not to die for your country, but to make the other poor bastard die for his." The point of meme warfare is, conversely, to make the 'other poor bastard' unwilling to die for his.[4]

FIGURE 18. Subvertisement by Greenpeace aimed at Exxon.[5] *Source:* Used with permission by Greenpeace.

Smart mobs can also use countercultural means to effect social change and corporate social responsibility. Anticorporate "subvertising" (as compared to advertising) is one such approach, where corporate brands are spoofed and reappropriated in ways that subversively lead to social change and question the basic integrity of the brand.

Another approach to meme warfare is "shop-dropping," which is the opposite of shoplifting. Instead of stealing from a store, urban street artists are now bringing in cans and boxes to display on the shelves. Imagine armies of smart mob organizers who shop-drop local stores with a particular message to disrupt normal practices. Meme warfare in the future will attempt to undermine ideas and social practices in ways that challenge the underlying beliefs of a society.

A Smart Mob Leader

One of the most successful smart mob organizers is Jimmy Wales, creator of Wikipedia. Wales started with a clear, compelling, and rather outrageous vision: to reach everyone in the world with a free encyclopedia for all human knowledge. As with any good intent statement, he had great clarity about where he wanted to go, but great flexibility with regard to how to get there.

Wales clearly envisioned Wikipedia as a social experiment built upon an existing technology platform that would be extended. Wikipedia is much more of a social innovation than a technological one. He clearly saw himself as a community organizer like Saul Alinsky, but with a different goal in a different medium. Volunteer editors enter and maintain the encyclopedia entries, but anyone can revise and update them. The editors watch the pages closely, however, and mistakes are usually corrected within minutes. Wikipedia has become a great place to start a research project, even though it would be a mistake to end there.

The Wikipedia vision took a smart mob to implement, and it takes many smart mobs to maintain it now that it has grown to such a massive scale. It is evolving into a permanent smart mob, a community others can build upon, or what we call in the next chapter a commons.

Smart Mob Organizing Summary

Smart mob organizing is an important ability for leaders of the future. I began using group communication through computers (similar to what we now call a wiki) with small groups of scientists and engineers in 1972. After I facilitated those early online conversations, I realized that I did not have the ability or the patience to be a smart mob organizer myself. Still, I saw its value and I have always worked with people who have these skills. Leaders do not have to do everything themselves.

My point is not that all leaders need to be smart mob organizers personally—although it is better if they use the media themselves and do at least some of their own organizing. Rather, it is that all leaders must be respectful and understanding of their importance in the future when they will all need to have smart mob organizers working for them. A.G. Lafley at P&G, for example, makes frequent use of the Internet to share his message, but he does not always make the entries personally. Leadership cannot only be expressed face-to-face or through broadcast media—it must be expressed through the web. Leaders must be smart about which medium works best to deliver the message at hand. Smart mob organizing is a skill that all leaders must utilize in order to make the future.

Commons Creating

Ability to seed, nurture, and grow shared assets
that can benefit other players—
and sometimes allow competition at a higher level.

THE MORE CONNECTED you are, the freer and safer you are. Connectivity can only make you free and safe, however, if you nurture it. As a planet, we are searching for new common ground. What is it that we have in common that could make the world a better place for more people?

New commons are shared resources that create platforms for generating wealth and value. Commons grow out of connectivity.

As we move into the next decade, expect a wide range of new commons structures. Consider these diverse examples from today's world as prototypes for where we will be going.

- Svalbard International Seed Vault: a storage facility built into a mountain near the North Pole, the vault was created and is supported by the Global Crop Diversity Trust and the Norwegian government. It opened in early 2008 and is a commons dedicated to the preservation of crop diversity for future generations.

- Ponoko: an online site that builds products one at a time from user designs. Users can buy, sell, create, and customize their designs. Thus, Ponoko has become a commons for open source design.

- Unified Grocers: a California-based cooperative that distributes food for retailers up and down the West Coast of the United States. Unified is owned by its members and is structured to benefit them all. It is a traditional food cooperative that is transforming itself to a new model of commons creating—to allow more advanced forms of competition that build upon shared resources.

Future leaders will be called to create new commons, to grow new places within which collaboration and mutual success can occur. There will be many opportunities to create new commons between public and private, social and economic, digital and physical. These spaces and places present many leadership challenges because they will be full of dilemmas, some of which will appear hopeless on the surface.

Essentially, the search for new commons is a process of engaging with dilemmas that combine what is good for both the individual and the community. Is it possible to address personal needs and community needs simultaneously? In a world shaped by problem-solving mentalities, having a winner usually implies that there is a loser as well. However, in a world of dilemmas, the potential for win/win solutions is more apparent, if leaders can figure out ways to flip the dilemmas into opportunities.

Peter Barnes describes this space between public and private as the "third economic sector" in his book *Capitalism 3.0*.[1] This title is an example of dilemma flipping itself. Capitalism as currently defined

FIGURE 19. The Svalbard International Seed Vault a storage facility, built into a mountain near the North Pole. *Source:* Used with permission, Svalbard Global Seed Vault. Mari Tefre, photographer.

has an inherent tension between the public and private sectors. This is not a problem that can be solved, but a dilemma to be flipped. The balance could be better or worse—depending on your point of view. *Capitalism 3.0* brings new web networking language to a very old concept—to reframe how we view capitalism. This juxtaposition should start an interesting conversation.

Traditional capitalism assumes that narrow self-interest is the driver. Barnes understands the pressures of profit in capitalism, but he challenges unexamined assumptions and creates a space for exploring beyond the traditional balance of power between public and private sectors. It is in this space that interesting new approaches to leadership will occur over the next decade in the world of new commons.

InnoCentive, NineSigma, and YourEncore provide a commons exchange for scientific consulting. Each of these efforts started as a smart mob, but evolved into an ongoing commons aimed at sharing R&D resources organized in a network similar to eBay.

Maker Faire has become a kind of commons for makers, a place for them to convene and share what they do. More importantly, it is a place where makers learn from each other. Every maker is part of a network and the Maker Faire celebrates and amplifies those networks. Leaders can use commons events like the Maker Faire to prototype their own ideas. I expect that is why Microsoft sponsors an entire pavilion for makers who hack Microsoft products in creative ways.

Before hacking became a negative term, it described ingenious individuals who pushed the technology to its extreme and came up with imaginative new uses or ways of using. Hackers pushed the edges, building better systems by breaking the old ones and rebuilding them. They blaze a trail for the rest of us. Increasingly, instead of litigating against them and policing their customers who "misuse" their products, companies are rewarding hackers who come up with new ideas. Hackers are prototypers in disguise for the next generation of products and services. They also help explore the possibilities for creating new commons, including shared resources for the hackers themselves.

In the past, the notion of a commons often referred to the village green or "Tragedy of the Commons," in which individual self-interest in grazing one's sheep led to collective disaster, since there was not enough grass for everyone if all the sheep took their fill.[2] This was a world of clearly limited resources and a self-contained system that was very difficult to grow.

In the future, we will have limited resources in some domains, but we will also be able to shift resources from one area to another. New network-amplified commons will allow new opportunities for win/win solutions and new potentials to synchronize individual self-interest with larger common interests. New commons create new clarity with regard to sharing resources and rules for engagement. Traditional notions of individual self-interest will expand. Competition will still be important, but in a new context that can make it even more profitable.

It will take genuinely creative thinking for leaders to identify potential new commons opportunities both within and outside of their own organizations.

Commons Creating Defined

A commons is a shared asset that benefits multiple players, as in shared wealth. If a team improves its playing field, all the teams that play there will benefit.

There are many different kinds of commons, including parks, town squares, beaches, and markets. While many commons are clearly organized for the public good, market-oriented commons are focused on providing a platform of shared assets that allow competition to take place at a higher level.

The term "commons" may not immediately bring to mind what I am trying to convey. A business term like "shared assets" might fit better, but I keep coming back to the aspirational notion of a commons. We need to learn how to create new commons that are beyond stereotypes and oversimplifications.

What is it that organizations and people could share in order to make all of their lives better? A commons is a platform on which individuals and groups can build for the greater good. The dilemma for leaders is to perform for their own organization while also growing a commons around them to benefit the surrounding community. For example, if a company does something that's good for both itself and the industry, the entire industry grows—not just one company.

There is fuzzy line between a smart mob and a commons. In general, smart mobs come and go. Commons, however, tend to have a long-term view toward sharing assets and continuing value for the participants over an extended period of time. Smart mobs can evolve into commons, but many of them are ad hoc. A market commons for people to buy and sell through the web, eBay also provides structures for evaluating buyers and sellers, so that fair exchanges can occur. It has become a very large commons platform that allows people to operate businesses and make purchases through the eBay protocols of exchange.

Leaders with strong commons-creating abilities will be able to mobilize shared resources. This vision of leadership is, in some ways, timeless and has always been a part of public and corporate life. In the networked age of the future, however, leaders will need to move beyond their own interests and beyond smart mob organizing to create new terms of engagement, new environments in which they can make the future they want to make.

Leaders will use smart mobs to build new collaborative structures, not just for the common good but to allow competition at a higher level—typically competition with profit margins higher than they were before the commons was created. The creation of a new commons can create new clarity within which both cooperation and competition can thrive. The commons game is not a zero-sum game, where some people must lose in order for others to win. In a commons game, win/win solutions are the goal. By expanding the playing field and upping the level of play, everyone could benefit.

Even though leaders are facing challenges of unprecedented scale, the tools and media for creating new platforms for cooperation are better than ever before. The tragedy of the commons will still apply in some cases, such as fishing in oceans, but the use of networks allow commons to extend win/win opportunities in new and exciting ways.

Commons creating is the culmination of all the other skills. Because it is complicated and there are many stakeholders, creating commons is often frustrating but also very satisfying for leaders who can do it. It is the most difficult and the most important future leadership skill, and it benefits from all of the other future leadership skills explored in this book.

Commons Creation in the Future

Leaders will have an opportunity in this next decade to reframe and broaden the purpose of their organizations. In the world of global interactive media, companies will have new potential to create both market value and more commons. Companies will be able to become stronger protectors of the commons that are already here and advocates for new commons that need to be created. Target, for example, already gives 5 percent of its profits to the communities where its stores are located. This is an example of contributing to commons that are already established locally, but what if that notion was extended to create new commons in areas like community economics or clean and affordable water? Business profits are important, of course, but long-term social profit is necessary for business to be sustainable. Inherent in creating commons is a leader's motivation to promote not only business profit but social profit as well. It is like a company providing an air purifier while also working at the commons level to create an environment where there is no need for them.

DIASPORAS AS COMMONS

Diasporas are a kind of commons by definition: they have strong shared values and common points of view on the world. Since sharing is already practiced regularly within their communities, diasporas can create new commons structures more quickly.

The challenge for diasporas is to grow new commons that extend beyond their own constituencies. While growing commons is typically easier within a diaspora, it is likely to be harder when it involves outsiders; or to express it in playground lingo, diasporas may not play well with other diasporas. They may develop commons for their own benefit, but they could exclude those on the outside, whether explicitly or implicitly.

One fascinating example of a commons geared toward diasporas is the Genographic Project by *National Geographic.* The project maps humanity's historical migrations, so that current diasporas can understand their histories better and new ones can be created based on ancestral DNA. As a planet, we have just shifted from being a primarily rural to a primarily urban place. Over the next decade, migrations will continue, including climate-induced migrations due to storms, earthquakes, and other shifts. The Genographic Project is one attempt to track the flow of DNA. The lesson: diasporas can be sustainable if they come up with a commons that preserves their basic values.

GOVERNMENT-SUPPORTED COMMONS

In recent years, Brazil has become a fascinating case study of government support for seeding the open source movement. This shift to increased transparency is writ large with the move from Microsoft software to Linux software in many quarters. Microsoft's source code is not open, meaning that it remains the property of its developers, and cannot be studied or changed. There is a cost for purchasing the software, and usually charges associated with upgrades. In contrast, Linux's open source software is free; it is also much more transparent and accessible. Some see this as a much-needed balm that would help to close the rich/poor divide between areas that are technologically enabled and technologically deprived. Sérgio Amadeu, author of *Digital Exclusion: Misery in the Information Era,* argues that governments should phase out closed source software in government work and invest in developing open source software, which can be fueled by Brazilian ingenuity, thus creating a kind of commons around open source software that benefits the entire economy of Brazil.[4]

There are other leaders in the open source movement in Brazil. For example, Ronaldo Lemos is known for his work with the national body of Creative Commons, which envisions a continuum of copyright options beyond closed ownership of intellectual property. With Creative Commons licensing, information may be designated as "some rights reserved" or completely in the public domain. Depending on the kind of Creative Commons license, information can be built upon, altered, or redefined by other users of that information. Lemos is also a pioneer of Overmundo, a Web 2.0 tool for collaborative community reporting of local cultural news. Articles undergo a peer review process by contributors and are voted on before they are published.[5] Overmundo gives voice to cultural perspectives that would otherwise have gone unheard and does so in a way characterized by active engagement and participation in shaping the stories.

OPEN LEADERSHIP COMMONS

Amy Schulman is a leader in the practice of law. Formerly a partner at DLA Piper and currently working for Pfizer, Schulman is a commons creator.[6] Known for her ability to build the right team for a project, Schulman is strong at cultivating mutual benefit and allowing competition at a higher level. She listens to her team and draws on them based on what she hears. Her colleagues say, "Amy is a very good listener and understands what her own strengths are, and in turn where she might have weaknesses that will not help with a particular problem. She is good at finding others to fill in for those weaknesses."[7]

Nurturing others through mentoring is another way that she engages with commons creating. For example, she organized a gathering of female attorneys to focus on career advancement. Heidi Levine, a younger associate, describes how Amy coached her on the mechanics of the law, but also on business strategy: "Learning directly from her helped me to grow in a way that I would not have otherwise experienced that early in my career. I have tried to pass that along to the women I work with. People, especially one's supervising partner, are usually hesitant to share that type of information as it could make them vulnerable. But Amy did, and in my eyes, it made her much stronger."[8] Through her efforts to stimulate advancement for others, she created a commons, a shared space in which both mutual benefit and greater responsibility occur.

Commons creating is the work of leaders, but these leaders are not necessarily always found at the top of an organization. Sometimes commons creating is unexpected and can come from the lower ranks. What is really crucial here is that the leader step back to create a space and to hold that space for the common good in an act of open leadership. This will allow others to enter and fill that space.

This kind of commons being created from below is evident at the beginning of Schulman's career when she was at the law firm of Cleary Gottlieb Steen & Hamilton based in New York. She went from a summer associate position to a full-time assignment where she soon bore responsibility for individual state cases for a large international client. Her role involved coaching local lawyers, many of whom were older and more experienced than she was, so the job required interpersonal skills and sensitivity to their situation.[9] Consensus building appeared more and more crucial to her as she learned how to build teams and get them to perform at their best.[10] She was not focused solely on her own performance, but on stimulating and growing the team.

FINANCIAL INNOVATION

Some financial institutions are examples of commons, such as credit unions or those banks focused on particular communities or purposes. Indeed, financial markets are, in some sense, commons—although most of these commons are geared more heavily toward individual greed that social profit.

Home mortgages began as commons when communities started banks to share risk and make loans to local people so they could build houses and businesses. Now, however, home mortgages have been packaged and resold as instruments for short-term trading. It is more challenging to find financial commons that support local communities.

The money commons idea is not dead, however. The Lending Club, for example, is one of several new social lending networks where members can borrow and lend money among themselves at better-than-market interest rates. These networks are creating new models for entrepreneurs who are interested in doing well while doing good, through commons-based services.

Another approach is being developed by Kiva.org, which combines the practices of microlending and commons creating. Muhammad Yunus, whom I referred to earlier in reference to his clarity, created new commons to enable very small loans to people (mostly women) who were part of communities where paying back the loan became a social responsibility. Yunus and his microlending philosophy have had major impacts on local communities through a very large number of very small loans. Kiva has now created an online structure that allows anyone online to be a Yunus-like social investor. Kiva provides arm's-length structures through the web where specific individuals can request specific loans. Contributors decide who they want to lend to, agree upon terms for repayment, and follow the progress of the loan through Kiva. Kiva gives contributors a way to lend to a specific entrepreneur in the developing world, to help empower that person to work him- or herself out of poverty. These are one-on-one personal loans, through the Kiva commons structure.

SOME COMMONS EXAMPLES

Since commons creating is the most difficult future leadership skill, I provide here a range of examples that are consistent with future directions in IFTF Ten-Year Forecasts. Of course, there are traditional commons that should be considered, such as the European Union, the United Nations, and NATO. But the next generation of commons will be different. Consider these examples, some of which may not use the word "commons" to describe their activities:

- MDVIP: a for-profit network of physicians, who have restructured their practices to limit the number of patients per doctor (to allow for more personal consultation) and provide services geared toward healthy living for a monthly fee. MDVIP is a business based on the foundation of shared health resources across a dispersed network.

- OScar: a project that functions like a commons to develop different cars from the same base of open source standards and materials. Their goal is to break away from the constraints of the current automobile industry and reinvent mobility, using open source principles.

- COMPASS: Communication Partnership for Science and the Sea is a collaborative effort of scientists to bridge the fields of marine conservation science, public interest, and marine policy. Their focus is on marine ecosystem services and ecosystem-based management. The oceans border many different countries, and COMPASS is one attempt to bridge the different interests.

- The Wild Farm Alliance (WFA): This is an agricultural commons effort to protect and restore wild nature, envisioning "a world in which community-based, ecologically managed farms and ranches seamlessly integrate into landscapes that accommodate the full range of native species and ecological processes."[11] This is what I think of as a restorative commons, with an eye to the future.

This short list of future-oriented commons efforts is only intended to be illustrative. The very concept of a commons will evolve over the next decade, with lessons from past efforts being transformed into very new kinds of commons organizations and networks. Leaders will have a chance to connect and build common platforms in ways that have never been possible before.

Commons Creating Summary

We are a broken planet, but not a planet without hope. We are facing major challenges of global climate change, pandemics, bioterrorism, and other stark realities. Every generation seems to think that its prospects are worse than those of any previous generation, but arguably, the future appears more threatening now than at any other time in history. Our connectivity, however, is our strength. Leaders will have new opportunities to create commons that address the challenges. The more connected we are, the safer and the more powerful we are—if we realize our interconnections. Through the growing global electronic webs, we are able to communicate and cooperate better than ever before. The next decade will be both a frightening time and a hopeful time.

The ten new leadership skills described in this book all build on each other, from the maker instinct on through clarity, dilemma flipping, immersive learning, bio-empathy, constructive depolarization, quiet transparency, rapid prototyping, smart mob organizing, and finally commons creating. The order is intentional, building from instinct to action. Making comes from an inner urge. Commons creating is extremely complex and delicate. The maker instinct is where the commons are rooted: the urge to grow a sustainable shared wealth. Commons creating requires dilemma flipping and engagement with polarized conflict, but the best leaders will see through the mess with a clarity that articulates the essence of the commons they are trying to create. Nature provides insight regarding commons; in nature, commons are called ecologies. Transparency is required, but self-promotion is dangerous. Leaders will have to rapid-prototype their way to their new commons, using smart mob organizing techniques that have the promise to become sustainable. These ten skills will give leaders a great chance to make the world a better place—in spite of the many challenges.

As we think about and plan for the future, children are what we all have in common. Children keep us humble, especially those of us who are parents. The next generation will be the focal point for new commons. Thinking about the world we want to leave for our children and grandchildren gets everyone in a good space to create a commons and make the future.

In the VUCA world of volatility, uncertainty, complexity, and ambiguity, these ten future skills will be basic to successful leadership. The broken planet issues will be daunting, but networked connectivity will create incredible opportunities to make different futures that heal and remake our broken planet.

Readying Yourself for the Future

Leaders can make the future.
Leaders can decide what kind of future
they want to create and go for it.

GIVEN THE FUTURE FORCES of the next decade, where do you stack up in terms of your current leadership skills? Are you ready to lead in a future that will be volatile, uncertain, complex, and ambiguous? How could you improve your own readiness?

This final chapter will help you rate your own readiness for the future—given the forces of the next decade—as well as draw some conclusions about leadership in the years to come.

Leadership Questions to Ask Yourself

Looking back at the ten core chapters, you now have an opportunity to assess your own readiness for the future. Don't consider this assessment absolute, since nobody can predict the future. Rather, use it to spark your own thinking about leadership and how you might like to develop yourself as a leader in the future. You have to decide what kind of leader you will want to be, but challenges from the future can bring out more of your own innate leadership gifts. I believe that there will be many new skills for future leaders to learn.

First, answer the questions below as candidly as you can. I have grouped the questions around the ten future leadership skills, each of which was described in an earlier chapter. Review the chapters if you need to as you answer these questions for yourself. They are intended to help you personalize the ten future leadership skills and point to how they might apply to your own leadership development.

I realize that these are personal questions. Leadership begins from the inside, from your own values and point of view. Leaders can make a better world, but it will take an inner balance and personal discipline. Please ponder these questions and think about them personally as you reflect back to the ideas in each chapter. These are meant to be discerning questions, but you need to decide what they mean for you. These questions are designed to help you assess your own leadership skills and where you might need to improve.

CHAPTER 1: DO YOU HAVE A *MAKER INSTINCT*?

- When you were a child, think back to the ways in which you played in sand or the dirt. What kinds of things did you make? What did you enjoy the most? How has this experience contributed to your leadership style as you have matured?

- How would you describe your interests as an adult in *how* things work, beyond just what gets produced as output? How does this interest translate into your own leadership style and skills?

- How do you express your own do-it-yourself urges to cook, sew, knit, work with wood, design, write, or do other tasks where you are either making or remaking? How do these instincts contribute to your role as a leader? Are there ways you could bring these skills to work more often?

- What do you learn from reading *MAKE: Magazine, Technology Review,* or some other maker publications? Do you participate in online discussions about making? What have you learned in exchanges involving people who make things? How is your exposure to other makers contributing to your own leadership?

CHAPTER 2: DO YOU COMMUNICATE WITH *CLARITY?*

- Think back to a recent meeting in which you had trouble getting your point across. What were the characteristics of that situation? How did you respond as you tried to be clear? Would the people you lead describe your leadership as clear?

- How often have you been complimented about your clarity in expression in any medium? Think of some specific examples. How do you express clarity in purpose through your leadership? Is your intent clear to those you lead?

- How would you express your own personal leadership legacy in a single compelling sentence? What leadership skills will be most important in order for your legacy to be successful?

- How would you express your organization's Strategic Intent or Winning Proposition in a single compelling sentence? How do your leadership skills contribute to that winning proposition?

CHAPTER 3: CAN YOU *FLIP DILEMMAS?*

- Think about a specific dilemma you have faced in your recent experience. When you could not solve it, how did that make you feel? How did you respond? How did you explore ways to flip the dilemma around so that it could become an opportunity?

- Do you get energized when you are in the midst of doing a puzzle, before you solve it, or even if you cannot solve it? How do you apply that energy to explore ways to flip dilemmas into opportunities as part of your leadership?

- Are you willing to decide and move ahead when a decision needs to be made, even when you don't have a solution? Think of a decision you've had to make where there was no apparent solution.

- Think of a case where you were able to flip a dilemma into something positive. What leadership skills did you demonstrate in doing this? Where might you be able to improve?

CHAPTER 4: DO YOU HAVE AN *IMMERSIVE LEARNING ABILITY?*

- Do you seek out new experiences from which you could learn—especially situations that make you feel uncomfortable? Think of a recent example and how that experience has contributed to your leadership.

- Have you recently immersed yourself in a different world in order to learn? What did you learn? How did that learning get expressed in your leadership?

- How are you interested in the experience of and lessons of new video games? Do you seek to understand how serious and casual gamers are playing?

- How have you participated in management games or simulations in your organization? Would you be willing to do so if someone else suggested it? Do you encourage the use of gaming and simulation as a learning medium?

CHAPTER 5: DO YOU HAVE *BIO-EMPATHY?*

- As you were growing up, did you live in or frequently visit outdoor spaces like forests, oceans, farms, ponds, or parks? How did you play outside in nature? How does this experience contribute to your leadership today?

- Do you have an emotional need to be in natural settings frequently and learn from the experiences you have in nature? How do you satisfy that need? How does this emotional connection to nature contribute to your leadership?

- When you were in school, were you attracted to biology, life sciences, zoology, geography, anthropology, or other similar courses? Do you think of yourself as an amateur or professional life scientist, biologist, geographer, or natural scientist?

- How do you look to nature for insight about challenges you have in your life? How do these life lessons get translated into your leadership style and skill set?

CHAPTER 6: CAN YOU *CONSTRUCTIVELY DEPOLARIZE* A SITUATION?

- How are you able to look at the world through the eyes of others, including those who make you feel uncomfortable? How do you express your curiosity about other cultural practices that are different from your own? Can you give some recent examples?

- How do you listen and learn from people who come from unfamiliar cultures where you have little experience? Are you judgmental about cultural habits and practices that do not conform to your own values?

- Have you traveled internationally as a way of learning about people who think differently from you? When you do travel, do you seek out opportunities to learn how people in other cultures live? Do you speak multiple languages? If so, what have you learned about constructive depolarization by thinking across languages?

- Think of an example where you have calmed a polarized situation and constructively engaged people toward some new path forward. How did you respond? What worked? What did not work?

CHAPTER 7: DO YOU HAVE *QUIET TRANSPARENCY*?

- How do you share your reasons for doing things with others, especially with those whom you are leading? Would the people you lead characterize you as quietly transparent?

- How do you express trust toward others—particularly people you are leading? Do the people you lead feel that you trust them? How do you embody this trust in your leadership style?

- Do you have a strong need for others to recognize your accomplishments? Would the people you lead say that you have a strong need for personal recognition? Can you think of a recent experience where you demonstrated quiet transparency in your leadership, showing both strength and humility?

- Has anyone ever referred to you as humble? What do those situations where you have shown humility have to say about your own leadership?

CHAPTER 8: CAN YOU DO *RAPID PROTOTYPING*?

- Are you anxious to try out things as soon as possible in order to learn what works and what does not? Give a recent example of when you have done this as part of your role as leader.

- Early on in a new task, do you get frustrated or impatient if things don't work right away? If so, how do you work through that frustration?

- Think of an example where you kept trying out different approaches to a new idea over and over again, in a rapid prototyping process. What did this experience reveal about your own leadership style? What additional skills could help you do this better?

- What is an example where you were able to learn from your own failures? How does your approach to "failure" fit in with your own leadership style? Do you encourage people you lead to learn from their own failures?

CHAPTER 9: CAN YOU DO *SMART MOB ORGANIZING*?

- Do you find it satisfying to bring together groups of people? What are recent examples where you have done this? What aspects of this process do you find most satisfying?

- Do you like to reach out and network with others, both in person and through online media?

- Do you have a personal rule of thumb with regard to which medium is best for a given situation?

- Are you able to use online social media in your role as leader? Have you practiced your leadership skills through a range of different media? How does your use of online media leadership compare to your in-person leadership?

CHAPTER 10: CAN YOU DO *COMMONS CREATING?*

- Do you seek out and try to create situations where multiple parties benefit (as opposed to a situation in which you alone win)? Can you give recent examples when you have tried to do this, whether or not your efforts were successful?

- Have you ever given anything away in order to get more in return? Think back and describe how this process worked. Was it a win/win situation in the end?

- Have you read about historical efforts to create commons that reward both individuals and larger groups? What lessons do you take away from these historical experiences? What is different about the new commons?

- Do you like to read fantasy fiction or scenarios about how things could be or might be in the future? What writing do you find most relevant to your own leadership?

Rate Your Own Leadership Skills for the Future

The questions above are personal warm-ups for you to rate yourself on the ten future leadership skills. Please rate yourself on each of the future skills below, according to the following criteria:

VERY STRONG:	+2
STRONG:	+1
UNCERTAIN:	0
WEAK	−1
VERY WEAK:	−2

_____ *Maker Instinct:* exploit your inner drive to build and grow things, as well as connect with others in the making.

_____ *Clarity:* see through messes and contradictions to a future that others cannot yet see. Leaders are very clear about what they are making, but very flexible about how it gets made.

_____ *Dilemma Flipping:* turn dilemmas—which, unlike problems, cannot be solved—into advantages and opportunities.

_____ *Immersive Learning Ability:* immerse yourself in unfamiliar environments to learn from them in a first-person way.

_____ *Bio-Empathy:* see things from nature's point of view; to understand, respect, and learn from nature's patterns.

_____ *Constructive Depolarizing:* calm tense situations where differences dominate and communication has broken down—and bring people from divergent cultures toward constructive engagement.

_____ *Quiet Transparency:* be open and authentic about what matters to you—without advertising yourself.

_____ *Rapid Prototyping:* create quick early versions of innovations with the expectation that later success will require early failures.

_____ *Smart Mob Organizing:* create, engage with, and nurture purposeful business or social change networks through intelligent use of electronic and other media.

_____ *Commons Creating:* seed, nuture, and grow shared assets that can benefit other players—and sometimes allow competition at a higher level.

The range of total scores for rating your future leadership skills runs from minus 20 to plus 20. As you interpret your own self-ratings, consider the following:

A total of plus 20 would mean that you have a perfect set of leadership skills to match external future forces over the next decade as forecasted in this book. You are ready for the future, according to your own self-rating. Would others (especially people you lead) agree with your self-rating?

A total of minus 20, on the other hand, would mean you are a perfect misfit for the future. You have a lot to learn to get ready to lead in this future. Or perhaps you are forecasting a different future? Or perhaps you are being overly humble or too hard on yourself?

Workshops Using the Ten Future Leadership Skills

The ten future leadership skills are designed so that they can be used in workshops, not just for self-assessments. For example, I often use the ten future leadership skills in workshops as a way of linking the Ten-Year Forecasts I am presenting to the individual leaders in the room—and to the leaders as a team. What are the most important leadership skills for a particular organization to consider? This is a discerning question for leaders to pause and consider.

The questions at the front of this chapter are good for reading in advance or starting a discussion to get people familiar with each future leadership skill. Reading this book in advance, or as a follow-up, can also help get people oriented to the future leadership skills so that they can engage with them and apply them.

I have tried to create titles for the ten future leadership skills that get people's attention without turning them off. People and cultures vary, however, and some terms communicate better than others for particular groups. It is a good idea, after working with the skills for a while, to ask the group what skills are missing. The ten future leadership skills are meant to be provocative but not exhaustive. Sometimes, letting groups identify and name their own future leadership skills could work better than staying with my list. Perhaps my list will inspire a group to come up with others that are better suited to them.

It is important to remind workshop participants that they do not have to agree with these ten leadership skills to find them useful. Looking at the list may prompt leaders to articulate leadership skills that are unique to their own environments but not fully expressed in the ten skills described in this book.

I have used the ten skills with many groups, and I'm convinced that they are constructively provocative for a wide range of leaders. My goal in presenting the ten future leadership skills is to spark conversations about future leadership in a very personal and practical way.

Often, I ask groups of leaders to do their self-assessments before I present the Ten-Year Forecast. Sometimes I ask them to assess their team. When I'm working with a graphic artist, I use a simple show of hands and the artist creates a quick histogram of the leadership team's skills.

I like to ask leaders to choose the top four leadership skills (out of the ten) that they believe they already have as strengths. If they feel they are strong in more than four skills, I ask them to choose the top four that best describe their current leadership skills. If they say there are fewer than four skills at which they feel strong, I ask them to just select those they are already good at. Every leadership team has some areas where it already feels strong. It is very interesting to see which skills are most attractive to a particular leadership team and which are most foreign. Each time I've done this exercise with a leadership team, we have gotten an interesting distribution of skills and a great conversation has ensued.

The best workshops involve some form of immersive learning experience. IFTF has designed a game that immerses leaders in the VUCA world to give them a firsthand taste of each of the future leadership skills. In this context, participants self-organize based on their top leadership skill scores and complete missions that draw on certain combinations of skills. This gives them a chance to practice the skills in a low-stakes way and to determine what areas of transfer there may be to their high-stakes business environments.

Most of the leadership teams I work with are not very strong on bio-empathy, for example. That is an area where many decide they need to improve. Many of the teams with whom I work come from engineering backgrounds, so bio-empathy is not comfortable for them—unless they have also had experiences in nature as they grew up.

Also, most leaders today consider dilemma flipping very tough, since they were trained to be problem solvers and that's how they got to where they are today. Many still believe they can problem-solve their way to success in the VUCA world. They don't want to hear about problems that they cannot solve or that won't go away. Problem solvers are likely to be very frustrated in the future if they are in top leadership positions. Many problem solvers refuse to believe they have anything to learn.

Finally, commons creating is a skill that seems most unusual to today's leaders, but will be mandatory for leaders of tomorrow.

I have also found it useful to present the ten future leadership skills at the beginning of a workshop, before I dive right into the Ten-Year Forecast. The discussion about the forecast often links back to the leadership skills. Toward the end of the workshop, I ask participants to review their self-ratings, since they will then have a much better understanding of the skills after having a while to think about them and apply them in the context of the Ten-Year Forecast. Their final ratings are usually much more useful than the ones they did at the start. It takes a while for people to get comfortable with the ten future leadership skills and to draw similarities and differences to their own leadership styles.

Take a Personal Look Back and Look Ahead

As you look forward to your own leadership in the future, I recommend that you look back at your life and the choices you have made. Your past shapes your future, but there are also opportunities to break out of your own pattern. Understanding where you have been is an important part of determining where you want to go and what you need to learn. The ten future leadership skills are meant to be provocative, to cause you to consider your own leadership skills and think ahead to the next stage in your professional life. There may be parts of your own background that you want to revisit and perhaps resurrect as part of your leadership style. On the other hand, there may be things you need to unlearn or change. As in any effort to think systematically about the future, it is important to look much further back than you are looking forward and to think personally about your own experiences as a leader and the choices you have made.

I got to meet the management visionary Peter Drucker late in his life. When asked about leadership and how to create an organizational climate that can help leaders grow, he advised that people try out many roles in life and work with many different types of people when they are young (essentially using rapid prototyping), since they don't yet know who they are. In the second half of life, he said that people should only work on things they are passionate about and with people they admire. I found this very optimistic advice, since Drucker lived to be ninety-five and worked productively up to the end. What Drucker saw as the first half of life—almost fifty years— allows leaders a lot of time to take on different identities and seek their own styles of leadership. It also gives all of us time to learn leadership skills like those introduced in this book.

Each of us has taken steps toward leadership from early in life, even if we don't realize it. As an undergraduate at the University of Illinois in Champaign-Urbana, for example, I led a protected life as a college basketball player on scholarship. Since Illinois was a land grant college, I was required at that time to take part in the Reserve Officer Training Corps. When the John F. Kennedy was killed in 1963, we were ordered to march around in a vacant field—with nobody watching. Thinking back, that experience was an important part of my leadership learning.

As best I can tell, marching was an attempt to put order around the disorder that had shaken us all. We were doing something familiar in a situation that was suddenly unfamiliar: our president had been killed. We were marching to bring back our sense of order. With this experience, I got an early taste of how leaders respond to volatility, uncertainty, complexity, and ambiguity. 1963 was a simpler time—or at least it felt that way to me.

I had another leadership moment of truth in graduate school. It was a big identity shift for me to go from thinking of myself as a basketball player to thinking of myself as a serious student. I found myself very attracted to studying the future, but it was hard to know where to start and how to engage. I have a vivid memory of the exact moment I first learned about Institute for the Future. As a research assistant in divinity school, I was in my professor's office and looked down on his table and saw an article in a new publication called *The Futurist*. (See Figure 20.)

I was frozen in place. "That's where I'd love to work," I thought with a clarity that I didn't even know that I had.

Seeing that article about the Institute for the Future was a major

Vol II, No. 4, August, 1968

Institute for the Future
Will Begin Operations
In Connecticut this Fall

A newly-formed Institute for the Future, which will seek to organize systematic and comprehensive studies of the long-range future, will establish its eastern headquarters this September in Middletown, Connecticut.

Facilities will be established later on the West Coast and in the Southwest, according to current plans.

President Frank P. Davidson said the IFF would develop the nation's first comprehensive computer-oriented system for predicting and controlling the long-range impact of technological and economic change. An urban research laboratory will be developed as a first priority project.

FIGURE 20. A 1968 clipping from the *Futurist* announcing the formation of Institute for the Future. *Source:* Used with permission from the World Future Society (wfs.org).

turning point in my life, although I didn't realize it until years later. I had an immediate attraction to thinking about the long-term future, but it took me some years to develop a leadership role in that space. In 1972, at the conference in Washington, DC, where the ARPAnet was publicly introduced, I presented a paper based on my dissertation at Northwestern. By good fortune, I was on a panel with a senior researcher from Institute for the Future who invited me to apply for a job. I got the job and, remarkably, I am still working at IFTF thirty-five years later, immersed in my fifth different career there.

I am very fortunate that I have been able to work on things I am passionate about since I first came to Institute for the Future in 1973. My leadership roles at IFTF have varied, but it has become a home where I can thrive. By Drucker's criteria, I found my calling early—well before my life was half over.

My leadership lessons from early life helped me figure out what I could do and what I could not. As I went on in graduate school and continued to try out different roles, I gradually figured out what I could do well—and how I wanted to continue to learn. Each leader has to figure out a path that works for him or her. My experience was a form of prototyping for me, although it was not that rapid. I was practicing for the life I am now living.

Leaders are likely to do better in situations they have experienced before, in situations for which they have practiced. Once in a VUCA situation, leaders will be disoriented. The discipline of practice and preparation (immersive learning ability) really is useful *before* a crisis so that decisive action can happen rapidly—especially in situations where there is no time to consider all the options. The challenge, of course, is to simulate experiences that will be useful in the future worlds. Leaders don't want to be caught playing out-of-date games in new situations that demand new approaches.

Once you are in an uncertain world, you may not have much time to think—you will immersed, like it or not. Clarity becomes extremely important in crisis situations. In my days as a basketball player, for example, I often found myself flipping back and forth mentally between playing and watching myself play, or thinking about what I needed to do next or the consequences of missing a shot at a critical time. I learned to my surprise that I could actually shoot *better* without my glasses. Seeing details (basket, crowd, cheerleaders) caused me to lose my focus. Without the detail, I could get into the flow of the game more much easily and my muscle memory allowed me to shoot well even when I could not see well.

This dilemma has continued through my life, particularly in writing and public speaking. If I start thinking about what I'm writing or what I'm saying, I can lose the flow. Certainly, we all need to reflect periodically. Too much reflection, however, can mean we are not prepared to act, to decide when we need to decide. All leaders are challenged by the dilemma between staying in the moment and stepping back to assess how things are going.

It is great to try out lots of different leadership roles until you find one that really fits for you. Rapid prototyping is wonderful—especially when you are young. Daniel Seddiqui is an extreme example: he was in his mid-twenties and had a hard time finding a full-time job. He came up with a clever alternative: finding lots of one-week jobs to grow his experience base, since most employers wanted people with experience. He found a series of fifty jobs in fifty states, working one week on each.[1] He wrote a blog to record his experiences, which are now incredibly broad for someone who has never had a full-time job. Now that is rapid prototyping. Along the way, he developed a good sense of what he would like to do on a more permanent basis. This kind of creative turnaround is exactly what leaders need to do in the VUCA world.

While I was writing this book, I taught a workshop on senior leadership development for Chevron. Also on the program was Robert Rosen, author of *Just Enough Anxiety*.[2] Even the title is a gift for leaders. Expectations are so important and so fragile. Leaders should expect anxiety and seek out situations that have "just enough" of it to fuel their own leadership.

Volatility, uncertainty, complexity, and ambiguity are not new. Everyone experiences moments in life that have all of these characteristics. My long experience as a Ten-Year Forecaster leads me to believe that the future will be more volatile, more uncertain, more complex, and more ambiguous. To understand the future leadership skills at the core of this book, it helps to look at these emerging principles that form a profile for future leadership.

VOLATILITY YIELDS TO VISION

Leaders need a compelling sense of the future they want to create. In a world of dilemmas, future intent is needed to provide a sense of focus and grounding. Bio-empathy helps to shape leadership vision, since natural principles provide important clues about where to go and what to avoid. Leadership vision must include a quest for new commons—new shared assets that a wider community can use in constructive ways. Leadership vision, however, should be carried out with your own personal style of quiet transparency and strength.

UNCERTAINTY YIELDS TO UNDERSTANDING

Leaders need to immerse themselves in the cross-cultural worlds they will be serving, and they will need to listen and learn in order to figure out how to turn around the dilemmas they will face. Immersive learning ability will be critical to understand worlds that are unfamiliar and possibly threatening. Some situations will need to be depolarized before any progress can be made. Bio-empathy can help, since natural principles often yield new insights about what's really going on. Finally, the maker instinct provides curiosity to spur leaders on to a better understanding of what's going on and how things can be improved.

COMPLEXITY YIELDS TO CLARITY

Since clarity will be rewarded even if it is wrong, leaders need to be not only clear, but trustworthy, accurate, and transparent. The urge for clarity will seduce people toward polarities and extremes because absolute statements are comforting and are usually stated with great confidence. Clarity must be both compelling and simple—but not simplistic. Bio-empathy can help leaders make sense out of complexity and find a deeper clarity in the principles of nature. The best leaders will express clarity calmly and quietly yet powerfully in ways that people find meaningful. They will need to be very clear about the commitments they are making and the commitments they seek. There is a big difference between leadership clarity, which asks for commitment, and blind faith, which demands obedience. Shouting commands will not be enough.

AMBIGUITY YIELDS TO AGILITY

Leaders need great flexibility within the frame of their vision. The best ones will have great agility making the future. Indeed, all ten of the future leadership skills require agility in order to bring them to life:

- The maker instinct encourages an ongoing cycle of new projects, which needs an agile mind to orchestrate them all.
- Clarity is like the martial arts principle of being centered in the pit of your stomach, so you can respond with agility to attack.
- Dilemma flipping depends upon the agility of absorbing and reacting with creativity—without stumbling.

- Immersive learning ability often leads to disorientation, and you will need agility to recover your balance in the new setting where you are learning.

- Bio-empathy teaches agility in the form of resilience, a basic principle of successful natural systems.

- Constructive depolarization, which often necessitates delicate footwork, will be mandatory to cope with the extreme polarities of the future.

- Quiet transparency, a nimble balance of strength and humility, is the best leadership style for the future.

- Rapid prototyping is all about agility and learning on the fly. The best leaders will be perpetual prototypers.

- Smart mobs require dexterity to grow organically in the midst of fluid times, using various media.

- Commons creating demands a certain deftness to stretch into complex new territory where there can be multiple winners and shared assets.

Conclusion

Leaders need to understand all of these future leadership skills, but don't need to do them all at once or all by themselves. These ten skills are challenging to master, but each of them can be learned and there are many resources.

Maker instinct is the most personal of the skills, and it is certainly necessary to make and remake organizations. Clarity is also very personal, but others can help you shape it. You can start dilemma flipping based on your own view of the world, but others can help a lot in this area as well. All the other leadership skills can be shared with others, as long as the leader understands and believes in the approach. Bio-empathy, for example, can spread across the organization, but it will not work if the leader tries to control things in mechanical and linear ways. Leaders do not need to do all the smart mob organizing themselves, but they must set the vision and encourage the organizers—who must take on the authority to act.

Foresight is the ability to look over the horizon and see the big picture. It requires a combination of the maker instinct, clarity, and dilemma flipping—but the other leadership skills will contribute as well. All effective leaders must have the ability to think ahead, beyond the standard planning time frame. Thinking ten years ahead will give you a much more robust perspective from which to make decisions today.

Insight is discernment, the unique "Aha!" that suggests what it is that you should do to succeed. The ability to understand how your organization can make a difference comes from a creative combination of immersive learning ability, bio-empathy, constructive depolarization, and quiet transparency. A forecast, whether or not you agree with it, is a great way to provoke thinking, which can lead to insight. In the next generation of the Internet age, everyone will know what's new. The challenge for leaders will be to derive insight from the messiness around them and sense what's important.

Action depends upon the ability to decide on a strong path ahead. It requires rapid prototyping, smart mob organizing, and the ability to create new commons. Again, all ten future leadership skills will contribute to a leader's ability to act. Leaders may be known by their vision, but their actions will be evaluated most vigorously.

The best future leaders will have their own styles of cycling continuously through foresight, insight, and action. This book gives you the skills to do just that.

Moving from the negative VUCA (volatility, uncertainty, complexity, and ambiguity) to the positive VUCA (vision, understanding, clarity, and agility) will be the ultimate challenge for leaders in the future. As leaders of the future, you will need to have all ten of the future leadership skills in a mix that is all your own. Connectivity will bring the leadership skills to life and amplify their impact.

Leaders will make the future, but they won't make it all at once and they can't make it alone. This will be a make-it-ourselves future.

APPENDIX

Rate Your Own Leadership Skills for the Future

Try rating yourself on each of the future skills below, according to the following criteria:

VERY STRONG: +2
STRONG: +1
UNCERTAIN: 0
WEAK   −1
VERY WEAK: −2

_____ *Maker Instinct:* exploit your inner drive to build and grow things, as well as connect with others in the making.

_____ *Clarity:* see through messes and contradictions to a future that others cannot yet see. Leaders are very clear about what they are making, but very flexible about how it gets made.

_____ *Dilemma Flipping:* turn dilemmas—which, unlike problems, cannot be solved—into advantages and opportunities.

_____ *Immersive Learning Ability:* immerse yourself in unfamiliar environments to learn from them in a first-person way.

_____ *Bio-Empathy:* see things from nature's point of view; to understand, respect, and learn from nature's patterns.

_____ *Constructive Depolarizing:* calm tense situations where differences dominate and communication has broken down—and bring people from divergent cultures toward constructive engagement.

_____ *Quiet Transparency:* be open and authentic about what matters to you—without advertising yourself.

_____ *Rapid Prototyping:* create quick early versions of innovations with the expectation that later success will require early failures.

_____ *Smart Mob Organizing:* create, engage with, and nurture purposeful business or social change networks through intelligent use of electronic and other media.

_____ *Commons Creating:* seed, nurture, and grow shared assets that can benefit other players—and sometimes allow competition at a higher level.

The range of total scores for rating your future leadership skills runs from minus 20 to plus 20. As you interpret your own self-ratings, consider the following:

A total of plus 20 would mean that you have a perfect leadership skills match with external future forces over the next decade, as forecasted in *Leaders Make the Future.* You are ready for the future, according to your own self-rating. Would others agree with you about your self-rating of your own future leadership skills?

A total of minus 20, on the other hand, would mean you are a perfect misfit for the future as it is described in this book. You have a lot to learn to get ready to lead in this future. Or perhaps you are forecasting a different future? Or perhaps you are being overly humble or too hard on yourself?

These skills come from *Leaders Make the Future: Ten New Leadership Skills for an Uncertain World* by Bob Johansen (Berrett-Koehler Publishers, 2009), where they are described in detail. Also, up-to-date forms and resource materials to support the use of these future leadership skills are available at IFTF.org.

NOTES

Preface

1. The VUCA world terminology was developed at the Army War College in Carlisle, Pennsylvania. I learned about it when I was there the week before 9/11/2001. After 9/11, the Army War College started referring to itself informally as "VUCA University."
2. Bob Johansen, *Get There Early: Sensing the Future to Compete in the Present* (San Francisco: Berrett-Koehler, 2007).
3. The Ten-Year Forecast is an ongoing research program led by Kathi Vian at Institute for the Future. See http://www.iftf.org for details.
4. Institute for the Future published a map to the 2008 Maker Faire; it is published under a Creative Commons license available to everyone. David Pescovitz and Marina Gorbis were the lead authors, and this map was part of IFTF's Technology Horizons Program. See http://www.iftf.org to access and download the map.

Introduction

Epigraph: Confucius as quoted by James Geary, *Geary's Guide to the World's Great Aphorists* (New York: Bloomsbury, 2007), 72.

1. Johansen, *Get There Early*, 45-68. The original definition of VUCA was volatility, uncertainty, complexity, and ambiguity. In *Get There Early*, I introduced the idea of a VUCA turnaround with an emphasis on vision, understanding, clarity, and agility.
2. See http://www.nytimes.com/imagepages/2005/10/02/national/nationalspecial/20051002diaspora_graphic.html.
3. Governor of Massachusetts Deval Patrick attributed this phrase

to Barney Frank in a speech he gave on August 26, 2008. Full text available at http://www.demconvention.com/deval-patrick/ (accessed October 31, 2008).

4. William Gibson, "Broadband Blues," *Economist* 359, no. 8227 (June 23, 2001), 62.

5. This is a term from Linda Stone's work at Microsoft Research. See http://www.lindastone.net.

Chapter 1: Maker Instinct

1. See http://www.flickr.com/photos/pmtorrone/374863935/sizes/o/in/photostream/#cc _license by Creative Commons License http://creativecommons.org/licenses/by-nc-nd/2.0/].

2. See http://www.instructables.com.

3. Selected from the TCHO web site: http://www.tcho.com.

4. Wikinews, *Chicago chef invents edible menu,* Sunday, February 13, 2005. Accessible at: http://en.wikinews.org/wiki/Chicago_chef_invents_edible_menu (accessed October 31, 2008).

5. See http://www.cbsnews.com/stories/2007/06/03/sunday/main2878788.shtml (accessed October 31, 2008).

Chapter 2: Clarity

1. As I tell this story, I recall the early days of my career when business and government leaders were not allowed to make decisions in the first hours after international travel due to jet lag. International travel was longer and more difficult then, but some of the rigors of time shifting remain, and they certainly affect my mental state.

2. Apparently my experience was not unusual. I saw this article after I returned: "British Airways Worst for Losing Luggage," *Money Times,* August 4, 2007. Available online at http://www.themoneytimes.com/news/2007084/British_Airways_worst_for_losing_luggage-id-107545.html (accessed October 31, 2008):

> After losing more luggage than any other European airline, British Airways reportedly sought to keep its dubious No. 1 ranking under wraps. BA lost one bag for every 36 passengers in April, May and June—nearly double the European industry average of one lost bag for every 63 passengers," an Association of European Airlines (AEA) survey said.

British Airways asked the AEA not to make the data public out of fear it would hurt business, *The Times* of London reported Saturday. *The Times* said BA had so many lost bags piled at London's Heathrow Airport, it rented a fleet of trucks to haul the luggage to Italy for sorting. Some passengers said it took more than a month to get their belongings returned.

The AEA report also said nearly a third of British Airways' flights departed later than scheduled. Only three airlines scored lower than BA in that category—and they were much smaller, *The Times* said.

3. Gary Hamel and C. K. Prahalad, *Competing for the Future* (Boston: Harvard Business School Press, 1996), 141.

4. Willie Pietersen, *Reinventing Strategy: Using Strategic Learning to Create and Sustain Breakthrough Performance* (New York: J. Wiley and Sons, 2002), 42.

5. For more, see http://www.ogilvy.com.

6. For more, see http://www.southwest.com.

7. For more, see http://www.pg.com.

8. For more, see http://www.syngenta.com.

9. CPT Joel C. Dotterer, "Commander's Intent: Less Is Better." This quote is from Field Manual 100-15, 14 June 1993. Accessible at: http://www.GlobalSecurity.org (accessed on November 4, 2008).

10. See http://www.pbs.org/weta/carrier/ for a synopsis and video clips, as well as instructions for ordering the entire series.

11. Speech delivered on April 3, 1968, at the Mason Temple Church, Memphis, TN. To view a clip of this speech, go to http://www.americanrhetoric.com/speeches/mlkivebeentothemountaintop.htm.

12. Alan Jolis, "The Good Banker," *Independent* (May 5, 1996), http://www.gdrc.org/icm/grameen-goodbanker.html.

Chapter 3: Dilemma Flipping

F. Scott Fitzgerald as quoted by Edmund Wilson, ed. *The Crack-Up* (New York: New Directions, 1945), 69. I thank Nathan Estruth, leader of Future-Works at Procter & Gamble, for pointing me to this quote early in my writing of this book.

1. See Johansen, *Get There Early*, 74, for a longer description and analysis of modern dilemmas.

2. Lt. Commander Charles Swift, *Esquire*, March 2007, available at

http://www.esquire.com/features/ESQ0307swift?click=main_sr
(accessed October 31, 2008).

3. Roger Martin, *The Opposable Mind: How Successful Leaders Win Through Integrative Thinking* (Boston: Harvard Business School Press, 2007).

4. See http://www.selectminds.com.

5. Porter B. Williamson, *Patton's Principles: A Handbook for Managers Who Mean It!* (New York: Simon & Schuster, 1982).

6. Larry Huston and Nabil Sakkab, "Connect and Develop: Inside Procter & Gamble's New Model for Innovation," *Harvard Business Review* 84 no. 3 (March 20, 2006).

7. A.G. Lafley and Ram Charan, *The Game-Changer* (Crown Business: New York, 2008).

8. Winston Churchill quoted by James Geary, *Geary's Guide to the World's Great Aphorists,* 72.

9. Flip-flopping is usually a pejorative term to refer to changing one's position back and forth, often depending upon the audience. It allows politicians to be attractive to a wider range of people. Flip-flopping, or even the appearance of it, is something that politicians seek to avoid. There are cases, however, when what appears to be flip-flopping is actually an authentic dilemma flipping based on insight or a changing set of variables.

10. See Johansen, "What's Different about Dilemmas?" *Get There Early,* 69-84, for detailed discussion of distinguishing dilemmas from problems. See also "It Takes a Story to Understand a Dilemma," *Get There Early,* 87-100.

11. See Johansen, *Get There Early,* 78-81, for a fuller discussion of the threshold of righteousness.

Chapter 4: Immersive Learning Ability

1. Scott F. Dye, MD, "Conscious Neurosensory Mapping of the Internal Structures of the Human Knee Without Intraarticular Anesthesia," *The American Journal of Sports Medicine* 26, no. 6 (1998), 774.

2. See Constance Steinkuehler and Sean Duncan, "Scientific Habits of Mind in Virtual Worlds," *Journal of Science Education and Technology.* Accessible online at http://website.education.wisc.edu/steinkuehler/papers/SteinkuehlerDuncan2008.pdf. The authors downloaded the content of 1,984 posts in 85 threads from a discussion board for players

of *World of Warcraft*. I thank Zach Mumbach from Electronic Arts for pointing out this research to me and for reviewing this chapter as I was writing it.

3. Just google "Jane" and "games" to glimpse the range of her gaming activities, as well as see how a person with a great online identity presents herself without a business card. For more on this, see http://www.newyorker.com/online/video/conference/2008/mcgonigal and Jane's web site http://www.avantgame.com/.

4. See Johansen, "Immersion: The Best Way to Learn in the VUCA World," *Get There Early*, 101-21. This chapter provides more detail on the range of immersion experiences and explores how they can be used in the foresight to insight to action process.

5. Robert Johansen, Jacques Vallee, and Kathleen Spangler, *Electronic Meetings: Technical Alternatives and Social Choices* (Reading, MA: Addison-Wesley, 1979), Appendix. The boxed version of *Spinoff* is now out of print.

6. For details on the most recent online forecasting games, see the Ten-Year Forecast portion of IFTF's web site at http://www.iftf .org, and particularly this article on the first Massively Multiplayer Forecasting Platform: http://www.iftf.org/node/2319.

7. Sue Halpern, "Virtual Iraq: Using Simulation to Treat a New Generation of Traumatized Veterans," *The New Yorker* (May 19, 2008), 32-37.

Chapter 5: Bio-Empathy

Wendell Berry, "The Pleasures of Eating," *What Are People For?* (San Francisco: North Point Press, 1990). Available online at http://www .stjoan.com/ecosp/docs/pleasures_of_eating_by_wendell_b.htm (accessed November 4, 2008).

1. See http://www.polyfacefarms.com/principles.aspx (accessed November 2, 2008).

2. Essentially, they are grass farmers who just happen to produce other products from the grass, like meat.

3. Scott F. Dye, MD, "The Pathophysiology of Patellofemoral Pain: A Tissue Homeostasis Perspective," *Clinical Orthopaedics and Related Research* no. 436 (2005), 100-110.

4. Katherine Jefferts Schori, *A Wing and a Prayer: A Message of Faith and Hope* (New York: Morehouse Publishing, 2007), 8.

5. The forecast map and a video describing it are available on the GEMI Web site: http://www.gemi.org.

6. Operation Purple is run by the National Military Family Association and The Sierra Club. Please direct questions regarding Operation Purple to operationpurple@nmfa.org.

7. Ibid.

8. For example of how this phrase is in use, see this article from the *Journal of Soil and Water Conservation.* Available online at http://www.jswconline.org/content/63/5/149A.short (accessed November 4, 2008).

9. This course was taught by Professor Linda L. Golden, Marlene and Morton Meyerson Professor in Business, McCombs School of Business, University of Texas, Austin.

10. See http://www.syngenta.com/en/about_syngenta/visionandbusiness.html (accessed November 4, 2008).

11. I was told about this on a visit to Safeco Field on August 22, 2008.

12. See, for example, Dorling Kindersley's *Eyewitness Books* series. Some of these books are explicitly future-oriented, but all are solid introductions to science and nature. Reading children's books is a kind of do-it-yourself reverse mentoring. Available online at http://us.dk.com/nf/Search/AdvSearchProc/1,,S320,00.hl (accessed on November 4, 2008).

Chapter 6: Constructive Depolarizing

1. Robert A. Burton, MD, *On Being Certain: Believing You Are Right Even When You're Not* (New York: St. Martin's Press, 2008).

2. Edward T. Hall, *The Silent Language* (Garden City, New York: Anchor Press/Doubleday, 1959), 29.

3. Ian Wylie, "Meetings Resolve Almighty Issues," *Financial Times* (July 15, 2008). I was able to talk with a number of people about the Lambeth Conference, but I thought that this article about conflict management was a very good summary of the approach. It is fascinating that the *Financial Times* and Ian Wylie did this analysis, looking at Lambeth as a source of insight about conflict management in business. I thank Professor Ian Douglas for his review of this account of the Lambeth Conference.

4. Douglas Johnston, *Faith-Based Diplomacy: Trumping RealPolitik* (Oxford:Oxford University Press, 2003).

5. Beth Jones, "Queen Rania Takes on Stereotypes," *BBC News/Middle East* (July 25, 2008), http://news.bbc.co.uk/1/hi/world/middle_east/7524933.stm (accessed November 4, 2008).

6. See http://www.youtube.com/user/queenrania?ob=4.

Chapter 7: Quiet Transparency

1. See http://makezine.com/04/ownyourown/ (accessed November 1, 2008).

2. James Gilmore and Joseph Pine, *Authenticity: What Consumers Really Want* (Boston: Harvard Business School Press, 2008).

3. Michael E. Conroy, *Branded!: How the "Certification Revolution" Is Transforming Global Corporations* (Gabriola Island: New Society Publishers, 2007).

4. That said, her work takes root more broadly in the realm of changing workforce, changing family, and changing community.

5. See http://www.timberland.com.

Chapter 8: Rapid Prototyping

1. See http://www.au.af.mil/au/awc/awcgate/army/tc_25-20/table.htm (accessed November 4, 2008).

2. See http://www.grove.com for a description of the work of The Grove and for access to their visual templates.

3. Winston Churchill as quoted by James Geary, *Geary's Guide to the World's Great Aphorists,* 72.

Chapter 9: Smart Mob Organizing

1. Howard Rheingold, *Smart Mobs: The Next Social Revolution* (New York: Basic Books, 2003). Howard continues to be a thought leader in this field and a continuing source of inspiration.

2. See http://www.mdhealthevolution.com.

3. Vannevar Bush, "As We May Think," *Atlantic,* July 1945.

4. Richard Dawkins, *The Selfish Gene* (Oxford: Oxford University Press, 2006).

5. For more on this provocative campaign by Greenpeace, see http://www.greenpeace.org/usa/campaigns/global-warming-and-energy/exxon-secrets.

Chapter 10: Commons Creating

1. Peter Barnes, *Capitalism 3.0* (San Francisco: Berrett-Koehler, 2007).
2. Garrett Hardin, "The Tragedy of the Commons," *Science* 162 (1968), 1243-1248.
3. For more information, see http://www.cio.com.au/index.php/id;1491647901;fp;4;fpid;21;pf;1 or http://www.wired.com/techbiz/it/news/2003/11/61257 or http://www.nytimes.com/2005/03/29/technology/29computer.html.
4. For more information, see http://icommons.org/articles/web-20-in-brazil-the-overmundo-case (accessed on October27, 2008).
5. See http://blogs.wsj.com/law/2008/05/28/dlas-amy-schulman-lands-top-legal-job-at-pfizer/ (accessed October 29, 2008).
6. Boris Groysberg, Victoria W. Winston, and Shirley Spence, "Leadership in Law: Amy Schulman at DLA Piper," *Harvard Business Review* (Case 10.1225/407033), 5. Further, "the experience taught Schulman that . . . 'good leaders are actually consensus builders and work to elicit the best from their teams. It's not a solo star opportunity.'"
7. Ibid, 6.
8. Ibid, 5.
9. Ibid, 5, "Cleary was representing a large Japanese petrochemical company in a product-liability case when Schulman joined the firm. It was an unusual piece of business, and Schulman, who joined the case at the very beginning, ended up with a great deal of responsibility for such an inexperienced associate. Her role involved working on individual state cases, essentially having a series of apprenticeships with local trial lawyers. But she was also there to instruct the local lawyers, which required some interpersonal skills: 'I needed to be sensitive to their circumstances, to what it was like to have a second-year, Yale-educated Wall Street lawyer tell a trial lawyer in his 50s or 60s, who had tried many more cases than I had ever thought I would, how to do things.'"
10. See http://www.wildfarmalliance.org.

Conclusion

1. Ian MacKenzie, "Daniel Seddiqui Works 50 Jobs in 50 States," *Food for Thought* (October 7, 2008).
2. Robert H. Rosen, *Just Enough Anxiety: The Hidden Driver of Business Success* (New York: Portfolio, 2008).

BIBLIOGRAPHY

Ashby, Meredith D., and Stephen A. Miles, eds. *Leaders Talk Leadership.* New York: Oxford Press, 2002.

Barnett, Thomas P. M. *The Pentagon's New Map.* New York: G. P. Putnam's Sons, 2004.

Bell, Wendell, and James A. Mau, eds. *The Sociology of the Future.* New York: Russell Sage Foundation, 1971.

Bennis, Warren, and Patricia Ward Biederman. *Organizing Genius: The Secrets of Creative Collaboration.* Reading, MA: Addison-Wesley, 1997.

Burton, Robert A., M.D. *On Being Certain.* New York: St. Martin's Press, 2008.

Conroy, Michael E. *Branded!: How the "Certification Revolution" Is Transforming Global Corporations.* Gabriola Island: New Society Publishers, 2007.

Davis, Stanley M. *Future Perfect.* New York: Addison-Wesley, 1987.

———, and Bill Davidson. *2020 Vision.* New York: Simon & Schuster, 1991.

Dawkins, Richard. *The Selfish Gene.* Oxford: Oxford University Press, 2006.

DeGeus, Arie. *The Living Company.* Boston: Harvard Business School Press, 1997.

Drucker, Peter F. *The Future of Industrial Man.* New York: The New American Library of World Literature, Inc. 1965.

Friedman, Stewart D. *Total Leadership.* Boston: Harvard Business Press, 2008.

Friedman, Thomas L. *The World Is Flat: A Brief History of the 21st Century.* New York: Farrar, Straus & Giroux, 2005.

Fromm, Erich. *The Forgotten Language.* New York: Grove Press, 1951.

Geary, James. *Geary's Guide to the World's Great Aphorists*. New York: Bloomsbury, 2007.

Goffman, Erving. *Frame Analysis*. New York: Harper & Row, 1974.

Goldsmith, Marshall, Cathy L. Greenberg, Alastair Robertson, and Maya Hu-Chan. *Global Leadership*. Upper Saddle River: Prentice Hall, 2003.

Goleman, Daniel. *Emotional Intelligence*. New York: Bantam Books, 1995.

Greer, Scott. *The Logic of Social Inquiry*. Chicago: Aldine Publishing, 1969.

Hall, Edward T. *The Hidden Dimension*. New York: Anchor Press/Doubleday, 1966.

———. *The Silent Language*. New York: Anchor Press/Doubleday, 1959.

Halpern, Belle Linda, and Kathy Lubar. *Leadership Presence*. New York: Gotham Books, 2003.

Harman, Willis, Ph.D. *Global Mind Change*. New York: Warner Books, 1988.

Heider, John. *The Tao of Leadership*. Atlanta: Humanics New Age, 1985.

Heifetz, Ronald A. *Leadership without Easy Answers*. Boston: Harvard University Press, 2003.

Hock, Dee. *Birth of the Chaordic Age*. San Francisco: Berrett-Koehler, 1999.

Hoffer, Eric, *The True Believer*. New York: Harper & Row Publishers, 1951.

Jaworski, Joseph. *Synchronicity: The Inner Path of Leadership*. San Francisco: Berrett-Koehler, 1996.

Johansen, Bob. *Get There Early: Sensing the Future to Compete in the Present*. San Francisco: Berrett-Koehler, 2007.

Johansen, Robert, and Rob Swigart. *Upsizing the Individual in the Downsized Organization*. Reading, MA: Addison-Wesley, 1994.

Johansen, Robert, David Sibbet, Suzyn Benson, Alexia Martin, Robert Mittman, and Paul Saffo. *Leading Business Teams*. Reading, MA: Addison-Wesley, 1991.

Johnston, Douglas. *Faith-Based Diplomacy Trumping Realpolitik*. New York: Oxford Press, 2003.

Keen, Peter G. W. *The Process Edge*. Boston: Harvard Business School Press, 1997.

———. *Shaping the Future*. Boston: Harvard Business School Press, 1991.

Kelley, Tom, and Jonathan Littman. *The Ten Faces of Innovation*. New York: Doubleday, 2005.

Kelly, Matthew. *The Dream Manager*. New York: Hyperion, 2007.

Kidder, Tracy. *The Soul of a New Machine*. New York: Avon Books, 1981.

Kuhn, Thomas S. *The Structure of Scientific Revolutions*. Chicago: The University of Chicago Press, 1962.

Lafley, A. G., and Ram Charan. *The Game-Changer.* New York: Crown Business, 2008.

LeGuin, Ursula K. *Lao Tzu: Tao Te Ching: A Book about the Way and the Power of the Way.* Boston: Shambhala Publications, 1997.

Lencioni, Patrick. *Silos, Politics and Turf Wars.* San Francisco: Jossey-Bass, 2006.

Martin, Roger. *The Opposable Mind: How Successful Leaders Win Through Integrative Thinking.* Boston: Harvard Business School Press, 2007.

Maslow, Abraham H. *Toward a Psychology of Being.* Princeton: D. Van Nostrand Company, 1962.

Mathews, Ryan, and Watts Wacker. *The Deviant's Advantage.* New York: Crown Business, 2002.

Mills, C. Wright. *The Sociological Imagination.* New York: Oxford University Press, 1959.

O'Hara-Devereaux, Mary, and Robert Johansen. *Global Work Bridging Distance, Culture and Time.* San Francisco: Jossey-Bass, 1994.

Pietersen, Willie. *Reinventing Strategy.* New York: John Wiley & Sons, 2002.

Pinchot, Gifford, and Elizabeth Pinchot. *The Intelligent Organization.* San Francisco: Berrett-Koehler, 1994.

Pfeffer, Jeffrey, and Robert I. Sutton. *Hard Facts, Dangerous Half-Truths & Total Nonsense: Profiting from Evidence-Based Management.* Boston: Harvard Business School Press, 2006.

Progoff, Ira. *Jung, Synchronicity, and Human Destiny.* New York: Dell Publishing, 1973.

Rheingold, Howard. *Smart Mobs: The Next Social Revolution.* New York: Perseus Publishing, 2002.

———. *Virtual Reality.* New York: Summit Books, 1991.

———. The *Virtual Community.* New York: Addison-Wesley, 1993.

Rosen, Robert H. *Just Enough Anxiety.* New York: Penguin Group, 2008.

Schori, Katharine Jefferts. *A Wing and a Prayer.* Harrisburg: Morehouse Publishing, 2007.

Shostak, Arthur B., ed. *Putting Sociology to Work.* New York: David McKay Company, 1974.

Smith, W. Stanton. *Decoding Generational Differences.* New York: Deloitte Development LLP, 2008.

Sproull, Lee, and Sara Kiesler. *Connections: New Ways of Working in the Networked Organization.* Cambridge: MIT Press, 1991.

Sutton, Robert I., *The No Asshole Rule: Building a Civilized Workplace and Surviving One That Isn't.* New York: Warner Business Books, 2007.

Taleb, Nassim Nicholas. *The Black Swan.* New York: Random House, 2007.

Theobald, Robert. *Futures Conditional.* New York: The Bobbs-Merrill Company, 1972.

Tichy, Noel M., and Warren G. Bennis. *Judgment: How Winning Leaders Make Great Calls.* New York: Penguin Group, 2007.

Toffler, Alvin, ed. *Learning for Tomorrow: The Role of the Future in Education.* New York: Vintage Books, 1974.

Tohei, Koichi. *Aikido in Daily Life.* Tokyo: Rikugei Publishing House, 1973.

Vallee, Jacques. *Computer Message System.* New York: McGraw-Hill, 1984.

———. *The Network Revolution: Confessions of a Computer Scientist.* Berkeley: And/Or Press, 1982.

Watson, James D. *Avoid Boring People.* New York: Alfred A. Knopf, 2007.

———. *The Double Helix.* New York: New American Library, 1968.

Watts, Alan W. *The Wisdom of Insecurity.* New York: Vintage Books, 1951.

Wheatley, Margaret J. *Leadership and the New Science.* San Francisco: Berrett-Koehler, 2006.

Whitehead, Alfred North. *Science and the Modern World.* Toronto: The McMillan Company, 1925.

Williamson, Porter B. *Patton's Principles: A Handbook for Managers Who Mean It!* New York: Simon & Schuster, 1982.

Wilson, Edmund, ed. *The Crack-Up.* New York: New Directions, 1945.

ACKNOWLEDGMENTS

A lot of what I know about leadership I learned from Roy Amara, who was president of the Institute for the Future in 1973 and brought me to Silicon Valley to become part of the Institute. Roy passed away on New Years Eve, 2007. He had leadership qualities that I have come to think of as "Roy's gift" for future leaders. I started writing this book right after Roy's death. I feel called to share Roy's gift of leadership with future leaders, as best I can.

Roy was a very orderly thinker who focused on the disorderly future. He was a very strong leader in his own quiet and self-effacing way. Roy always treated people with respect, even if he disagreed with them. He encouraged spirited exchange of ideas at the Institute; there were—and are—many debates. But Roy wanted high conflict about ideas *and* high respect for people. The few times I saw him angry, he was still respectful to those who had upset him. Roy kept his commitments and had many long-term friendships. He was a leader that you could count on.

Roy Amara had an ability to be both strong and be humble—in the face of a complex future and an often-overwhelming present. The essence of Roy's gift is the wisdom to hold both of these abilities together. Roy's combination of strength and humility allowed him to engage with others who were very different from him. But Roy's gift also presents a dilemma for leaders: how can you be authentically strong *and* humble?

Roy Amara was both a leader and a maker. In a real sense, he made the Institute for the Future and he helped make or remake so many effective organizations with which he worked over his long career. *Leaders Make the Future* is dedicated to Roy Amara in the hope that we can all receive Roy's gift as we strive to make the future a better place.

All the royalties from this book will go to the Roy Amara Fund for Participatory Foresight, which is an initiative to bring Roy's gift to a much larger audience of people making the future.

I have many others to thank as well, beginning with my colleagues at the Institute for the Future. Marina Gorbis is our Executive Director, and she gave me complete support to embark on this volunteer effort at a time when the Institute was extremely busy with paying projects. Kathi Vian is the leader of the annual Ten-Year Forecast, and this book builds directly on that base of wisdom and foresight. As I mention in the preface, the ideas of both Jane McGonigal and Jason Tester were very constructive for me as I was writing. Thanks to Andrea Saveri for her great work on commons.

Rachel Lyle Hatch joined IFTF as I was writing the book and added so much to the project in so many ways. Rachel somehow manages to be a great content contributor, an extremely well organized person, and a positive life force all at once. My assistant Kathy Seddiqui helped clear the way for this project and manage it to completion while still carrying a full-time project load. Natalie Matzinger Fernández, a global business student from Brazil, did an internship with us and added a unique perspective at an important time for the book.

Berrett-Koehler is a very unusual publishing house. I have done books for large publishers and I have had several famous editors. Nothing in my experience, however, compares to the quality of the work at BK. My editor Steve Piersanti is by far the best editor with whom I have ever worked. In fact, Steve is the best editor I can imagine. I come away from each session with Steve exhausted, but inspired to take the manuscript to a new level. Rick Wilson was a great help with the cover and production. Indeed, I thank everyone at BK, since it seems like every single person gets involved with every book. I certainly feel supported as an author. Jeevan Sivasubramaniam assembles a remarkable group of reviewers who give constructively critical feedback. My reviewers for this book were Valerie Andrews, Danielle Scott, Frank Basler, and Douglas Hammer. Each provided great insight, in four very different ways. BK has a unique approach to external review and I find it extremely useful. I'm sure that this process has made this a much better book, and I hope I have lived up to their aspirations for the final product. Jim Levine of Levine Greenberg Agency is my agent. Jim has the insight of an author and the constructive guidance of a great agent. I am very grateful for both and for Jim's support. Tanya Grove and Dave Peattie at BookMatters did a wonderful job editing my manuscript.

While this book is about my point of view on leadership in the future, I have learned so much from my experiences at Institute for the Future. I am very grateful for this opportunity, which continues to be inspiring for me.

The current Board of Trustees at Institute for the Future is a wonderful mix of people that includes: Aaron Cramer, Steve David, Karen Edwards, Deborah Engel, Marina Gorbis, Ellen Marram, Bob Sutton, Kathi Vian, and Lawrence Wilkinson.

The current Institute for the Future team is the most exciting mix of people I have worked with in my thirty-five year history at IFTF. My sincere thanks to Richard Adler, Dawn Alva, Robin Bogott, Jeff Burgan, Jamais Cascio, Cesar Castro, Jackie Copeland-Carson, Mathias Crawford, Vivian Distler, Jake Dunagan, Zoe Finkel, Tessa Finlev, Rod Falcon, Lyn Jeffery, Marina Gorbis, Jean Hagan, David Harris, Rachel Lyle Hatch, Jessica Hemerly, Andy Lam, Kim Lawrence, Harvey Lehtman, Mike Liebhold, Karin Lubeck, Miriam Lueck, Rachel Maguire, Jane McGonigal, Lisa Mumbach, Sean Ness, Neela Nuristani, Alex Pang, David Pescovitz, Mani Pande, Lynne Postlethwaite, Eddie Ray, Kathy Seddiqui, Chuck Sieloff, Abhay Sukmaran, Chris Sumner, Jeannie Swanson, Rob Swigart, Jason Tester, Anthony Townsend, Jody Radzik, Kathi Vian, and Anthony Weeks.

INDEX

ABOUT THE AUTHOR

Bob Johansen has worked for more than thirty-five years as a forecaster. Focusing on the human side of new technologies, Bob was one of the first social scientists to study the human and organizational impacts of the Internet when it was called the ARPAnet. He also has a deep interest in the future of religion and values.

Bob served as the Institute for the Future's president from 1996 to 2004. Still on IFTF's board, he now spends most of his time with IFTF sponsors, engaged in writing, public speaking, and facilitating top-executive workshops across a wide range of industries.

He is the author or co-author of seven previous books, including *Upsizing the Individual in the Downsized Organization,* a guide for organizations undergoing technological change and reengineering; *GlobalWork,* a guide to managing global cross-cultural teams; and *Get There Early,* an introduction to the foresight to insight to action cycle that helps leaders engage with the future context in constructive ways.

A social scientist with an interdisciplinary background, Bob holds a BS degree from the University of Illinois, which he attended on a basketball scholarship, and a PhD from Northwestern University. Bob also has a divinity degree from what is now called Colgate Rochester Crozer Divinity School, where he studied comparative religions.

ABOUT IFTF

The Institute for the Future (IFTF) is an independent nonprofit research group in Silicon Valley. We work with organizations of all kinds to help them make better, more informed decisions about the future. We provide the foresight to create insights that lead to action. The Institute is based in Palo Alto, California, a community at the crossroads of technological innovation, social experimentation, and global interchange. IFTF was founded in 1968 by a group of former RAND Corporation researchers with grants from Arthur Vining Davis Foundation and the Ford Foundation to take leading-edge futures research methodologies beyond the world of classified defense work.

For more information, please visit http://www.iftf.org.

Berrett–Koehler
Publishers

Berrett-Koehler is an independent publisher dedicated to an ambitious mission: *Creating a World That Works for All*.

We believe that to truly create a better world, action is needed at all levels—individual, organizational, and societal. At the individual level, our publications help people align their lives with their values and with their aspirations for a better world. At the organizational level, our publications promote progressive leadership and management practices, socially responsible approaches to business, and humane and effective organizations. At the societal level, our publications advance social and economic justice, shared prosperity, sustainability, and new solutions to national and global issues.

A major theme of our publications is "Opening Up New Space." Berrett-Koehler titles challenge conventional thinking, introduce new ideas, and foster positive change. Their common quest is changing the underlying beliefs, mindsets, institutions, and structures that keep generating the same cycles of problems, no matter who our leaders are or what improvement programs we adopt.

We strive to practice what we preach—to operate our publishing company in line with the ideas in our books. At the core of our approach is stewardship, which we define as a deep sense of responsibility to administer the company for the benefit of all of our "stakeholder" groups: authors, customers, employees, investors, service providers, and the communities and environment around us.

We are grateful to the thousands of readers, authors, and other friends of the company who consider themselves to be part of the "BK Community." We hope that you, too, will join us in our mission.

A BK Business Book

This book is part of our BK Business series. BK Business titles pioneer new and progressive leadership and management practices in all types of public, private, and nonprofit organizations. They promote socially responsible approaches to business, innovative organizational change methods, and more humane and effective organizations.

Berrett–Koehler
Publishers

A community dedicated to creating
a world that works for all

Visit Our Website: www.bkconnection.com

Read book excerpts, see author videos and Internet movies, read our authors' blogs, join discussion groups, download book apps, find out about the BK Affiliate Network, browse subject-area libraries of books, get special discounts, and more!

Subscribe to Our Free E-Newsletter, the *BK Communiqué*

Be the first to hear about new publications, special discount offers, exclusive articles, news about bestsellers, and more! Get on the list for our free e-newsletter by going to **www.bkconnection.com**.

Get Quantity Discounts

Berrett-Koehler books are available at quantity discounts for orders of ten or more copies. Please call us toll-free at (800) 929-2929 or email us at **bkp .orders@aidcvt.com**.

Join the BK Community

BKcommunity.com is a virtual meeting place where people from around the world can engage with kindred spirits to create a world that works for all. **BKcommunity.com** members may create their own profiles, blog, start and participate in forums and discussion groups, post photos and videos, answer surveys, announce and register for upcoming events, and chat with others online in real time. Please join the conversation!